ON THE EDGE

Surfing Stories by John McLean

Copyright © John McLean 2004

Published by Winter Productions, 21 Wigmore Street, London W1U 1PJ, Great Britain
E-mail: jnmcl90@hotmail.com

ISBN 1 872970 17 6

Cover design: Daniel Harrison

Printed through Colorcraft, Hong Kong, for Winter Productions, 21 Wigmore Street, London W1U 1PJ.

BY THE SAME AUTHOR

Island of the Gods. 578 pages. Price: £7.

Adrian goes to Bali on a surfing holiday and falls in love with the beautiful Dayu. The story is packed with interesting characters, wild parties, strange Balinese customs and wonderful sessions in the waves at Kuta Reef, Padang Padang and Uluwatu.

Deep Inside 198 pages. Price: £5

A collection of eighteen short stories that cover many aspects of surfing – the camaraderie of the line-up, surf trips to exotic spots, beach life, localism, after surf activities and other adventures. Funny, reflective, irreverent, stimulating and entertaining.

Down The Line 249 pages. Price: £6

Another collection of short stories that emphasise the beauty, freedom, fun and energy of surfing as well as the unique surfing lifestyle.

The Golden Few, 166 pages, Price: £5.

Ten year old Brett was born a thousand miles inland but tragedy and adventure combine to send him to the coast where he lives the idyllic life of a surfer and becomes one of the Golden Few.

Obtainable from leading surf shops or from: John McLean, 21 Wigmore St., London W1U 1PJ or P.O.Box 7135, Cloisters Square, Perth, Western Australia 6850 E-mail: jnmcl90@hotmail.com

CHAPTERS   **Page**

RANDY'S PARTY

The years that Randy spent at high school did not constitute the most glorious chapter of his life. He spent too many hours in the waves and too few in the classroom with the result that he did not exactly shine in the exams. However, he did have a good time.

Then there was his name. He had been christened "Andrew" but, by the time he had started high school, this had become "Andy". Then, as a result of his winning way with girls, he became known as "Randy Andy" and then simply "Randy".

When it came time for his interview with the school's "careers advisor" the sad faced little man just looked at the exam results and then at his chart and decided that there was no square hole that would fit this awkward round peg. Having been trained to look only at superficialities like exam results the man was inherently incapable of spotting the deeper things in Randy's make-up like his strong character, initiative and enterprise. "I really can't see you getting very far with the lack of effort you've shown so far. The future certainly does not look very promising," were the concluding words of the careers advisor.

"Not to worry," replied Randy cheerfully. "I usually find a way of getting what I want. It's worked with surfing and it's worked with girls. I don't mind what I do so long as I don't finish up a career's advisor."

"Cheeky young brat," thought the man as Randy stood up and walked out the door whistling a happy tune.

Upon leaving school at the age of seventeen Randy simply walked down the street from his home and, at the first building site he saw, asked if they needed an extra hand. He was immediately taken on as a brickie's labourer; for the next three months he worked in the sunshine, learned all about laying bricks and quite a bit more, built up his muscles and saved some money.

When the building was finished he took a couple of weeks off to go on a surfing trip and then started a new job, working for a landscape gardener. This too proved to be a learning curve and he grew to appreciate the plants with the love of the true gardener.

One of his father's friends at the golf club was building a new mansion and Randy's father arranged for Randy to do the landscaping in his off hours. This proved successful and led to more contracts and so he began working for himself, sometimes employing one or two of his surfing mates to give him a hand. When the waves were pumping they would down tools for a couple of hours and go surfing, making up the time by working later in the day or getting up earlier the next morning.

He even took a maintenance contract with the local council to keep the grounds around some of their buildings in order; in fact, so pleased was the council officer with the reliability and quality of the service, that he started to offer Randy more contracts and not all of them to do with landscaping. Randy always performed, expanding and contracting his flexible labour force as the work required. The council – and others – got their jobs done by young and nice looking surfers full of life and energy instead of the gnarled and lazy permanent workers that they had long been accustomed to. And, as an independent contractor, Randy was well on his way up the ladder of success.

It was shortly before his twenty-first birthday that, during a conversation with Mr. Jameson, the council officer, Randy learned that the old surf lifesaving club down on the beach was marked for demolition but so far the council had not been able to find a wrecking contractor.

A new clubhouse had been built at the other end of the beach and the old one had now been boarded up for two summers. "The problem is the price," said Mr. Jameson. "I would dearly love to let a contract this financial year but the budget does not extend to the five figure amount that a demolition contractor would charge. I know what their prices are like. It's still got water and electricity so all that would have to be disconnected too."

"Would you like me to have a look at it?" asked Randy.

"All right, but I didn't think that demolition was part of your business."

"Neither was landscaping or bricklaying before I took them up. And there haven't been any complaints, have there?"

"No complaints at all," replied Mr. Jameson as he handed Randy the key of the clubhouse.

After work Randy collected his girl-friend, Cynthia, and they went down to the beach to check the waves and watch the sunset. There were some nicely formed five footers rolling into the bay so Randy joined his friends for the dusk session. There were not too many in the line-up and he got some thrilling rides.

The last one took him right to the beach and so he joined Cynthia who was sitting on the sand. She towelled him down, combed his long, straggly hair and then massaged his tired joints.

Feeling refreshed, he led her up to the deserted clubhouse to have a look at its construction. When they unlocked the door they were assailed by a stuffy smell but, with the help of a torch, they found the light switch and turned it on. The building was not in bad shape, the big reception room and bar on the upper floor being exactly as Randy remembered them from the socials he had attended there from time to time. There was a bit of rot in the downstairs rooms but, he concluded, that would only make the task of demolition easier.

The next day he returned the key to Mr. Jameson and said ever so casually that, if the council was still interested, he would do the job for $5,000. "That is way below our estimate," said Mr. Jameson. "I don't want to see you make a loss on it. I can certainly let a contract for that price as we still have that sort of money in our budget. Are you sure you don't want to reconsider?"

"No, and I don't intend to lose on it. Just you wait and see."

The contract was duly signed, including a clause stating that the job had to be completed by the end of the following month which happened to be a week after Randy's twenty-first birthday. And another clause granted the demolition contractor the "full and exclusive use of the building before and during its demolition".

The next day he put a couple of his workers on the job – not to rip it apart but to do it up! He then sent out the invitations to his twenty-first. In the blank section for "Type of Party" he wrote "Rave" and for

"Place of Party" he wrote "the old surf club on the beach".

All the local surfers turned up with their ladies, their presents, their bottles of mineral water and other ingredients for an all night rave. It was a hot, windless night and by midnight the upstairs party room was buzzing with happy, sweating ravers and a thoughtful, sensitive, tuned-in DJ who somehow managed to give out the right sound at the right time. At least that is how it seemed. And perceptions are all that matter at a rave.

This was to be the last party in a surf club that over the years had seen many wild occasions and it seemed that all the good vibes of former times were concentrated in this one hot, intense and happy room.

"Hey, Randy, what are the waves going to be like to-morrow?" asked Robbie. "I can't see out of the big window. Too much steam on the inside."

Randy picked up a chair and threw it through the window, the tingling of the falling glass providing a contrast to the thump-thump of the techno like the sound of the triangles to the drum. "Ah, that's better," said Robbie as he peered out through the blackness towards the ocean. There were some big lines of white water rolling in from the deep. "Looks promising," he declared as he kissed his girl-friend and resumed dancing.

Randy was not as out of it as his window smashing behaviour might suggest. He had brought along a portable CD player to provide the sound for the short time that it would take to move the DJ and his gear from the upstairs party room to a small wooden platform on the sand a few yards further along the beach. And, of course, by then the happy ravers were too deeply into their dancing to notice the subtle change in the sound.

9

By 3 a.m. there was music inside the clubhouse – the CD player – and music outside on the beach – the DJ. Some of the surfers and their smiling, sweating ladies had moved outside where they danced under the stars with the waves in the background.

Inside the clubhouse Randy handed out a few hammers to the boys and they went around smashing windows, doors and the plywood partitions, the rhythm of their hammer thrusts being in tune with the music.

Randy then turned off the electricity and the whole of the clubhouse fell into darkness. The host pulled out of a cupboard some bales of hay which he had brought to the clubhouse earlier in the day. He untied them and, by the light of a couple of candles, he and all the others who were still upstairs started a first class hay fight, chucking clumps of the stuff at each other until the whole of the upstairs was knee deep in loose, dry, brown hay. The rave had turned into a barn dance with couples falling over on to the floor for a kiss and a "romp in the hay".

However, it was a case of *coitus interruptus* as Randy called out above the music for everybody to get out as the party would continue on the beach. Like sheep they all started filing down the darkened steps on to the sand. The last ones to leave saw Randy light a match and throw it on the hay. Whoosh! The barn dance was now a fireworks party as the flames rose up and devoured everything in their path.

With everyone now on the sand Randy and a couple of helpers cruised the downstairs rooms, scattering more of the hay and pouring petrol on it before lighting it. He had even gone to the trouble of making a small bomb which he lit and threw into the downstairs toilet. Boom! Even the loud techno was drowned out as that end of the building came crashing to the ground with red hot pieces of timber shooting into the air.

To keep the show going he threw a bag of fireworks into the blazing inferno. They all ignited within seconds and went flying off in all directions.

All dancing had now come to a halt as the partygoers stood and stared at the live pyrotechnic display that just seemed to get better and better. They stood as close as the heat would allow but even that was so hot that some of them had to take off all or some of their clothes. The bright orange of the flames appeared both powerful and beautiful as they rose in the darkness towards a moonlit sky.

The old wooden building creaked and crashed and burned for a couple of hours and by dawn there was only a low pile of still burning ashes and a few non-combustible materials that Randy would get his workers to remove on Monday, the wages for the estimated three hours' work and the truck trip to the dump being the only costs that he would have to outlay on his $5,000 contract.

As the sky became lighter the beach appeared different. And it was not just in the mind since the demolition of the two storey building had removed an accustomed landmark and allowed the great swathe of beach to be seen in all its space and glory.

In order to cool their excited and sweating bodies some of the partygoers ran into the sea for a swim. A few others, who lived nearby, went home and got their boards and before long one of the maddest surf sessions of all time was under way. Rave, barn dance, fireworks party, surf session - it seemed that nobody wanted this party to end. And when Randy saw one of the most experienced surfers in the bay trying to ride his surfboard upside down with the fins sticking up in the air he knew that his birthday rave must have been a success. With the old clubhouse down, the beach would never be the same again. Neither would the surfers.

A COLLEGE KID IN EUROPE

The Santa Barbara campus of the University of California sits on an isolated peninsula overlooking the blue Pacific. Because of its proximity to Rincon and other prime breaks it is favoured by surfers who like to combine their studies with the waves. It is also America's number one "party campus" where college kids have only a few short years to kick up their heels before moving into corporate jobs for the rest of their lives.

The exams had just ended and Tony was off to Europe for the summer. He had bought a cheap, "paid in advance" air ticket and would finance the rest of his travels by working at a "surf school" in the south-west of France for a month and by selling at a big profit the six brand new Al Merrick designed surfboards that he would be taking over with him for resale. They were packed in three big double board bags and were all ready to go with him to the airport.

On the eve of his departure the excited traveller met up with some of his surfing buddies on Del Playa Drive which, in the aftermath of exams, was one huge party scene where everyone seemed to be bronzed, blond and beautiful.

After a short time in this magnificent meat market Tony and his mates and a few girls went back to his apartment in Isla Vista for a final farewell.

From the top floor of his two storey pad one could see the ocean with the breaking waves in the foreground and the Channel Islands shimmering on the horizon. Towards sunset the partygoers all went up there to see what the surf was like.

"Of course, you get an even better view from the top of the roof," explained Tony. "But you have to climb out of my bedroom window and then up the steep pitch of the tiles to the top. It's quite a challenge."

"I always like a challenge," said Buck. This was the cue for the boys and girls to scramble out the window one by one, their cans of Bud in one pocket and more bud in the other pockets. The window and the top of the roof were safe enough but the bit in between was tricky. But they all made it in one piece and so the party continued on top of the roof where they felt closer to the waves and to the gods.

After a while Tony decided that they needed more refreshments and so, taking great care with his feet, he started walking down the sloping roof to the window. Unfortunately, just as he was in no-man's land in the middle – the part without any handholds – there was a good, old Californian earthquake which set the roof a-rocking and sent poor Tony skidding down the tiles. He tried to grab the guttering at the edge of the roof but the weight of his body and the speed of his fall caused it to come away and, like Tony, it went hurtling down to the concrete driveway below.

When the quake stopped Buck and Rod and the others very carefully made their way down the roof and in through the window, the screams of their friend having sobered them up more effectively than a cold shower.

Tony had two broken legs and some broken ribs. His head was undamaged but he was in excruciating pain. Fortunately, a drug dealer lived next door and so he came through the fence and gave him a shot of morphine which dulled the pain until the ambulance arrived.

14

Tony was able to talk to the others and one of his main concerns was the airline ticket on which he could not get a refund — not even for this type of accident — and all the surfboards in which he had invested his year's savings and which he knew he would not be able to sell in California for the big money he was expecting for them in France. Not to mention the position at the surf school that he had had such a hard job to score and he didn't want to let them down by not showing up.

"One of you will have to go on the trip instead and pay me back later," he cried. "Otherwise it's an empty seat on the plane. Both ways."

The only one who had not made plans for the long summer vacation was Rod who intended to surf Rincon for a couple of weeks and then think about getting a job. With his friend lying injured in front of him and the earthquake fresh in his mind he decided that perhaps a change of scene would be the answer. Rod had only ever been out of the United States once in his life and that was on a university debating trip to Vancouver the year before. So at least his passport was current.

After the patient departed Rod went up to the empty bedroom and found the tickets exactly where Tony said they were. He was still undecided when Buck burst in and said, "For God's sake, seize the moment, man. It's like seeing a perfect wave coming and not riding it. I'd go myself except I'm too deeply committed here work wise, woman wise and wave wise."

It was not until he was on his way to Los Angeles International Airport the next day that Rod looked at the route on the tickets and found that the destination was Amsterdam and not Paris. As he

15

thumbed his way through all the documents he discovered a Eurail pass and reasoned that that was how he would get to France for the surf school.

He breezed through the airport in Amsterdam with his eight surfboards – six of Tony's to sell and two of his own to ride. Since canals don't produce surf he left them in the Luggage Deposit while he went in to taste the pleasures of this city of beauty, youth and fun. It was filled with thousands of American college kids who, like him, had just finished their exams.

On his second night in Holland Rod went to a big "trance and dance" party in a small river valley where everybody seemed to be beautiful, loving and friendly. He was not just in a new continent but a new world.

The next step on this sudden surfing safari was the south-west coast of France. Rod and all his boards took up a sizeable part of the train that sped him down through the ancient heartland of France to Bayonne from where he took a bus up to Hossegor to present himself at the surf school.

This promised to be another new experience; after all, whoever had heard of a "surf school"? Rod and all his friends had taught themselves to surf by watching others and practising their manoeuvres. But if the French have courses in surfing like other countries have computer courses, who was he to complain? Especially when it was going to give him paid employment for a month. All he had to do was to say that he was Tony, do the work and receive the pay.

"But you are a week early!" exclaimed the "headmaster" of the surf school. "Your cabin won't be ready until I get back from Pamplona. Everybody is off

16

to Pamplona. I'm going down to-night; you can come with me if you like."

"Where's Pamplona?"

"Across the border in Spain. Where they have the running of the bulls. Hemingway and all that. You must have read about it."

They reached Pamplona about midnight and did the bars which, like Amsterdam, were full of that ubiquitous species, the American college kid.

Since this whole trip was one of rash decisions Rod decided to run with the bulls when the beasts were released into the confined streets of the old town the next morning. He donned the white cotton trousers, white shirt and red scarf for the dash through the streets with all the others and suffered a relatively minor cut on his upper arm from the sharp horn of a raging bull from which he managed to escape by his superb fitness.

"At least it proves that I ran with the bulls," he said proudly. "I just hope it doesn't heal until after I get home. After all, Tony will want to see my battle scars."

He found that the surf school for hopeless grommets was really a baby minding service so that the parents could go shopping but he did manage to sell all six of Tony's boards to various pupils whose parents paid him in the new "funny money" that the French now use as a replacement for their honourable franc.

Hossegor was like a month long party, both the waves and the bars being filled with – yes, you guessed – American college kids. So far Rod's wound from the bull had not healed and, with only another two weeks to go, he was already planning on how he was going to impress everyone back home with his souvenir of Pamplona.

When he received his final pay from the surf school he and some other college kids hired a car and drove down to a rock concert in San Sebastian, just over the border in northern Spain.

The next day he surfed Mundaca at six feet and then went to Guernica for a party night in the bars. He knew of this famous Spanish town from Picasso's great painting of its suffering during the Spanish Civil War. What he did not know was that Guernica was still the scene of a small and nasty civil war between the Spanish government and the E.T.A. terrorists.

His education in this particular subject occurred during dinner at the Las Palmas restaurant. Rod and his friends arrived shortly after 7 p.m. and sat down at the only vacant table which was at the end of a long, open air terrace. The place was filled with happy and very noisy diners and there was some Spanish music coming out of a stereo.

After sitting down and lighting their cigarettes, the guys had a look at the menu. They decided to start with a tureen of soup which was brought to the table by a smiling, bow-tied waiter. Perhaps it was his imagination but there did seem to be a split second of silence before the bomb went off at the other end of the terrace, shattering windows, bringing down walls, blowing off limbs and ending life.

However, by being so far away from the point of impact Rod and the others at his table were unharmed – at least physically. But it was not a nice sight to see the severed head of one of the waiters come hurtling through the air and land in the tureen of soup on the table. The splash of the hot soup on to their faces was the full extent of their injuries.

Amid the screaming of the dying and the sirens of the ambulances and police cars that were arriving on the scene Rod and his mates tended some of the wounded until the medics arrived. As he was lifting a woman off the floor Rod fell against a jagged piece of wall. This opened the small wound that he had received at Pamplona and it started bleeding.

With the emergency services assuming control Rod and the others decided to leave. As they were making their way over the rubble towards where their car was parked they saw a fat, red faced American reporter with a black briefcase who had just arrived with his panting cameraman.

"Are there any American college kids here? Any American college kids?" he was screaming. "We must have some bleeding American college kids for the evening news back in the States." Spotting Rod's long, blond hair and distinctive Anglo-Saxon features, the man rushed over and put his big, ugly mug in front of Rod's. "Are you an American college kid?"

"Yes, but I wasn't injured."

"Any of your friends injured?"

"No."

It was then that he saw a little bit of blood on the sleeve of Rod's white t-shirt from the opening of the Pamplona wound. "Look, you're bleeding!" he screamed. "You've been hit! The President might have to declare war. We can't have terrorists blowing up our college kids."

"I can assure you that this is an earlier wound," declared Rod.

By now the man and his assistant had grabbed Rod by the arms and were pulling him over the debris to a quiet corner. Still in the grip of the cameraman, Rod watched the reporter open his briefcase and pull out a large bundle of hundred dollar notes. "There's ten thousand dollars in this bundle and it's your's right now if you let us photograph that wound and say on camera that you received it in the blast."

"You are asking me to tell a lie for a piddling ten thousand dollars," exclaimed Rod with an air of disgust. "My usual rate for telling lies is twenty thousand dollars and not a cent less." Out of the briefcase came another bundle of ten thousand dollars.

Rod was then told what to say into the camera and to show his arm. For the final act he was told to break down so that no more words would come and then wipe away a fake tear or two – just like Clinton used to do when he went to funerals.

Rod had been in the university dramatic society and had taken a lead role in the production of Oscar Wilde's play, *The Importance of Being Earnest*, and so he knew how to carry on.

Even though it was evening he pulled out of his pocket a pair of John Lennon sunglasses and put them on. He then flicked his long, blond locks over as much of his face as they would cover and put on a strange face. "If they want me to do a Hollywood, I'll go the whole way," he decided. In short, he didn't want to be recognised by anyone back in Santa Barbara.

At the end of the interview, having done the fake tear and a little cry to Clintonesque perfection, he went to leave but the man called after him, "Oh, my God! In all the confusion we forgot to get your name and your home town."

"Bill Dixon from Jackson Valley, Oklahoma," he called out as he jumped into the rental car where his friends were waiting for him. Before he had even shut his door they were driving away from the scene of the drama as quickly as possible.

"Just keep driving!" said Rod. And they did. All the way to the Portuguese coast which they reached at lunch time on the following day.

They found a point break with a small hotel nearby and Rod used some of his newly acquired cash to pay their accommodation for the rest of the week.

The waves were clean and glassy as they broke over the sharp, rocky point and there was an old, crumbling castle on the hill above to provide a Crusader like background. Unfortunately, their nights were not so pleasant. Sleep was sometimes hard to find and, when it came, so too did the nightmares and they were always the same – that bloody waiter's head in the soup tureen. However, worse was to follow.

On the third night they drove into the local town for a bite to eat and a look around the shops. While the others were in a craftsman's shop, selecting some necklaces to take back to their girl-friends, Rod went off to buy a packet of Benson and Hedges at a convenience store. At the entrance to the shop were a couple of racks of newspapers. On one rack were the Portuguese papers while the other one showed the English language ones from Britain and America.

On the front pages of two of the American papers he saw a photo of himself; one was of his bleeding arm while the other showed his face but so good was his disguise that nobody would be able to recognise him. But it was the text that disturbed him the most. Under the headline "American Hero" he read, "Because nobody has been able to find Bill Dixon it is assumed that in his traumatised state he has either committed suicide or he has been captured and tortured by the terrorists who let off the bomb."

Further down he read that "this badly injured college kid" had been held up by the President as epitomising "the true spirit of American youth which in war and peace has been the greatest gift that God has yet bestowed on mankind".

Nor did the fact that there is no such place as Jackson Valley, Oklahoma, deter them as psychiatrists across the nation had declared that it would be expected that a traumatised victim would forget where he lived.

The article ended, "Step forward, Mr. Dixon, if you are still alive; the Congressional Medal of Honour has been conferred upon you. The President has said that he will travel 'anywhere, any time, any place' to pin the award on your sacred self."

This was dangerous stuff for someone who had only come to Europe on the spur of the moment for a surf and a bit of a party and so Rod decided to extend his holiday by another month until all the hoohaa died down. Having now experienced them both, he reckoned that the media were more dangerous than terrorism.

With the extra time he surfed some of the best breaks on the Portuguese coast and then went down to Anchor Point for a few days to experience the warmth and culture change of Morocco.

By the time he got back to Santa Barbara Tony was well on the way to recovery although he was still on crutches. "And how was the trip?" was the first question he asked Rod.

"Eventful."

When Rod handed over the price of the airfare plus what he got from the sale of the surfboards Tony thanked him and said that it would only partly pay the medical bills. "And I can't see how I can save up for a trip next summer as I won't be able to work for ages."

"You'd like to go to Europe next summer?" asked Rod.

"Of course, but it's only a dream."

"Listen, buddy, I made a little bit on the side while I was away. What say I put twelve thousand bucks into a bank account for us both to go to Europe next summer?'

"Are you serious?"

"Would I spin bullshit to you when it has the potential to disappoint?"

"Of course not."

Tony was stoked. He now had an added reason to get better and put his feet back on his surfboard to prepare for the surfing safari that had been so cruelly taken away from him by the fall off the roof.

He did not ask Rod where he got the money from for he knew that it is the etiquette of the waves never to ask a fellow surfer about newly acquired wealth that had been obtained "on the side". Just take it and enjoy it. And they did.

SURFERS AND CLUBBIES

Mussel Bay, on the coast of Australia, had an excellent beach break which made it a magnet for surfers. It also had some nasty rips which could be traps for the unwary. However, the local surfing crew – chaps like Bruce and Andy – knew where the rips were and, being experienced surfers and strong swimmers, reckoned that they were not in any danger.

This attitude was not shared by the "clubbies" from the surf lifesaving club at the southern end of the beach who were forever putting up red flags on the sand in front of the best surf spots and telling the surfers that they couldn't surf there because it was "out of bounds".

Most of the surfers just ignored them and paddled out anyway. This led to no end of trouble with the clubbies and the beach began to assume a cold war atmosphere. The loose living, disorganised surfers, who lived only for the waves, would gather at one end of the beach while the clubbies did their marching and lifesaving drills at the other end.

Even after dark the distinction was maintained with the lifesavers throwing wild parties in their clubhouse and the surfers gathering around a bonfire at their end of the beach. The surfers had long hair, the clubbies had short hair, the surfers wore long boardshorts while the clubbies got around in skimpy Speedos, the surfers smoked weed while the clubbies guzzled beer, the surfers had one kind of girlfriend while the clubbies had another. And so it went on – a thousand little differences and "never the twain shall meet".

Each group believed that they owned the ocean to the exclusion of the other. When the lifesavers

24

claimed that they were the ones who had to risk their lives to rescue those who got into difficulties, the surfers retorted that those who got caught in the rips were not surfers but inexperienced swimmers from the factory town a few miles inland.

As far as Bruce and Andy were concerned a clubbie was simply a pathetic little creature whose sole aim in life was to keep surfers out of their beloved waves while the clubbies regarded surfers as lawbreaking anarchists who represented all that was rotten in society.

Bruce had just turned twenty-four and had been going with Margie for a little over a year. She was petite with a perfect figure and long, blonde hair which fell to below her shoulders.

When he first met her he thought that she was the most gorgeous creature he had ever seen and, although he still felt deeply for her, he had become less and less demonstrative in his affections. In short he took her for granted. Of Scots-Irish descent, he had a wry sense of humour but a somewhat cynical outlook on life. More wit than charm and not really any conversation apart from the waves.

In the year plus since he met Margie he had put on a stone and a quarter in weight – mostly around his belly. He lived for surfing and, when he woke up at the crack of dawn each morning, his first thought was not of the beautiful lady lying next to him but of the waves; if the surf was up, he would leave her in bed and run down to the beach with his board.

She would see him when it suited him to come in; after a long session in the waves he would be as hungry as a horse and she would make him a big cooked breakfast for he was too lazy to cook for himself. He had also grown too lazy to shave each day – once or twice a week if they were going out and that was all.

On the warm days of summer Margie would accompany her "other half" down to the beach where he would go surfing and she would sunbathe topless on the sand. Because Bruce spent so much time in the water she developed the darkest tan on the beach and this only made her look even more attractive.

When he came in from a surf session Bruce's first question was always "Did you see that great ride I got?" or "What did you think of that last tube?" She always smiled and gave a positive reply even though, in nine cases out of ten, she had been dozing in the sun and dreaming of other things.

Sometimes Margie took her mobile phone to the beach and, while Bruce was carving up the ocean with Andy and the others, she would phone her girl-friends and have long heart-to-heart conversations as only girls can do. This usually provoked a typically sarcastic comment from Bruce about "women on the telephone" and all that sort of thing.

But to-day was not a mobile phone day; she had left it at home. After lying in the hot sun on her own for an hour Margie decided to cool off in the sea. That was about all she ever used the ocean for as she had never stood up on a surfboard and nor was she a strong swimmer.

She stood up, walked down the beach in her white g-string and immersed herself in the cool water. She was between the flags which the lifeguards had put up on the beach but, since it was a week day, there were not many swimmers in the water and, of course, Bruce and the other surfers were way out where the waves were breaking.

For about ten minutes Margie floated around, all the while keeping her lovely hair out of the salt water. Suddenly she felt a strong current that swept her a few yards further out but at an angle. She went to put her feet down at the bottom but couldn't. She then tried to swim back towards the shore but, despite a strenuous effort which even involved getting her hair wet, she made no headway.

Since there were so few people in the water her plight was spotted by the clubbie who was sitting in the chair at the top of the lifeguards' tower. He called down to his mate, Hugo, on the sand and pointed to what he called "a damsel in distress".

Hugo ran into the sea and, with vigorous strokes, swam out to where Margie was still struggling against the current. The young clubbie knew the rip well and had never regarded it as life threatening. He swam around it and came to Margie from the other side.

When he reached her he put his strong, muscular arms around her body and, taking her around the rip, brought her safely to the beach. Although not the most distressed swimmer that Hugo had rescued, she was certainly the most spunky. It was rescues like this one that made all those tedious hours of early morning drill on the beach worhtwhile.

With perfect poise she stood at the water's edge, tossed her hair into its rightful position and thanked Hugo for rescuing her.

He looked at his waterproof watch and saw that it was the time he came off duty so he asked her if she would like a cup of tea to calm her nerves.

"Thank-you," she smiled. "Where shall we go?"

"There's an urn at the surf club. Follow me."

The two of them walked along the water's edge, the one a suntanned goddess in a seductively cut g-string and the other a muscular, handsome youth with a "boyz band" face who was wearing a brief, tight fitting black swimsuit that revealed the outline of his manhood in obvious and distinctive fashion.

When they reached the surf club Hugo led her into the rather sterile "emergency room" on the ground floor. That was where the tea urn was and anyway, Margie was not allowed upstairs as that was "men only" – mainly because on hot days the lifesavers usually got around naked.

On the sand outside the emergency room was a small, round table and a couple of chairs and so rescuer and rescued sat down and sipped their hot tea.

With his olive skin Hugo's tan was even deeper than Margie's and at eighteen his chest was still hairless. "Do you go to the gym?" she asked as she observed his well-toned pecs.

"Occasionally," he replied, "but swimming usually achieves the same thing and it's much more fun. I don't like the smell of all the sweaty shoes at the gym. Why be inside when you can run and swim in the open air and absorb all the sunshine and beauty of the beach?"

"And what's it like to be a clubbie?" asked Margie as she thought of some of Bruce's more lurid descriptions of the hated species.

"Great. The surf club is a big part of my life. The patrolling of the beach is only the public part of it. That's when we're 'on parade'. Like soldiers defending a fortress, we are charged with the responsibility of

28

saving the lives of those who get into difficulties. Like the Army, we have our own drill and methods and everything is achieved by team work. Not like the surfers out there who think only of themselves." Margie kept her counsel and said nothing about Bruce or her own status as a "surfer's girl-friend".

"But, as I said," continued Hugo, "the public show is only one part of the job. Once we get back to the surf club and behind its castle like walls the fun really starts. It's like a complete community – but one that has a lot of fun. Up on the flat roof we have a deck where we can lie in the sun while the top floor has a bar, billiard table and kitchen. We often have all night parties and sleep at the club over week-ends. Nobody has more fun than clubbies."

"Not even surfers?"

"They don't even have a clubhouse for parties. Just an occasional bonfire in the wind and rain. Not my idea of fun." By now their bare feet were touching and Hugo's toes were resting on her's, sending some pretty powerful electricity through both their bodies. Margie could see that this confident young man had plenty of style and conversation and furthermore he had rescued her from the rip while her own useless boyfriend was miles out in the ocean and probably couldn't care less. At least that is what she told herself.

The more they talked the more interesting and attractive they became to each other and, of course, their feet were getting more playful than ever.

"To-night we're having a social at the club," said Hugo. "Would you like to come?"

"I didn't think women were allowed upstairs."

"They are if it is a designated 'social' and is after 8 p.m."

Curious to inspect the inner sanctum of "enemy territory" and keen to get to know Hugo more closely, Margie accepted.

"Great," he smiled. "I'll come and get you at your place. Where is it?"

"No, I don't think that would be a good idea; I'm in the same house as a surfer. At least for the moment. I'll make my way here and we can meet at eight."

"Fine. I'm staying in the clubhouse for the whole week. All I have to do is have a shower and shave and put on some clothes and come downstairs to greet you."

When they parted Margie gave him a kiss which she told him was for pulling her out of the sea. She couldn't help comparing his closely shaved chin with Bruce's prickly stubble.

She then made her way along the beach to where her boyfriend and Andy were sitting, their wetsuits rolled down to their waists and their long, straggly hair still dripping salt water.

"Where have you been?" asked Bruce who was surprised not to find her in her usual position on the sand waiting for him. Then, without waiting for an answer, he said, "Did you see that aerial I did about half an hour ago?"

"No, I've been at the surf club. I had to go along there for a cup of tea after I was rescued from the rip."

"But that rip's nothing," declared Bruce. "I've often been caught in it. So, some poncy little clubbie rescued you and took you for a cup of tea. How sweet!"

"Yes, he was rather. In fact, he's asked me to go to the social that they're having to-night in the clubhouse."

"And you said 'No'?"

"No, I said 'Yes'."

"So you're 'crossing the line'? The line that is written in sand and sea and stone and which has never been crossed before. And it's not going to be crossed to-night either."

"What do you mean?"

"I'm not going to let you go."

"You don't own me."

"You're a surfer's girlfriend; you don't go out with clubbies. Just as all their librarian-type girl-friends don't go out with surfers."

"I'll do what I like; I'm not some oppressed Moslem woman in a harem. And I'm sick and tired of all these rules and conventions on the beach. It's worse than the Catholic-Protestant situation in Belfast. And thanks for all the sympathy you gave me for being caught in the rip. Surfers are selfish and self-obsessed creatures. At least clubbies do something useful – like rescuing people from rips. And they look so cute in their little, sexy black swimming togs."

"Poofters – the lot of them," spat Bruce. "Marching up and down the beach like Nazis and dictating to us where we can surf and where we can't. If you go with that lot, no surfer would ever speak to you again."

"Well, they never seem to have much to say to me anyway. Just talking about the waves and nothing else."

"And what do clubbies talk about? The latest fashion in Speedos?"

"I'll find out to-night."

Margie arrived outside the clubhouse at five minutes to eight and a freshly showered and scented Hugo was there to meet her. He complimented her on her stylish white dress which looked wonderful on her tanned body.

"We can't go up yet," he explained. "We have to wait for the bell to ring at eight o'clock. You see, it's such a big thing to have ladies upstairs that a bell has to be rung to give them entry."

"You mean, to give some of the chaps time to put on their clothes?"

"Something like that."

At eight o'clock the bell tolled and Hugo led Margie and some of the other girls up the stairs. They were just in time to see a couple of bare butts running past the top of the stairs to the changing room to get dressed for the social.

The first thing that Margie noticed was that the music was very different from what was played around the camp fire at the surfers' end of the beach. And the amount of hearty beer guzzling suggested that the club was trying to get its name in the Guinness Book of Records. Yes, they were different but they made her welcome and Hugo was particularly attentive, charming and loving. At twenty-two she rather enjoyed being pampered by an eighteen year old hunk.

Back home Bruce was fit to be tied. He never believed that his girlfriend of more than a year would actually take herself to the lifesaving club. He thought it had all been bravado and it was not until Margie actually walked out the door and got into her car to drive away that he fully realised the enormity of what was happening. It was bad enough for her to leave him but to leave him for a clubbie was adding insult to injury.

Bruce and Andy opened a bottle of vodka and started drinking. The strong stuff gave them Dutch courage and they decided to walk down to the beach and see if her red Chevvy really was parked outside the surf lifesaving club.

They found it among the other cars and, not knowing which vehicle belonged to the insufferable little poseur who had lured her to the "other side", they let down the tyres of every parked car.

They could hear what they called "crap music" coming from upstairs as well as a lot of talk and laughter. Nobody was downstairs but they found that the door of the emergency room was open. They went in and Andy turned on the light switch.

On top of a table was the big tea urn and cups and saucers were strewn around. There was also a bed with a mattress for those who needed to recover after being rescued from the sea. Then Bruce noticed the club's switchboard and he decided to short circuit the whole building so as to destroy the party – no music, no ice and no lights. Ha, ha, ha! That would teach her and Hugo and all the other clubbies.

He fiddled about with the switches and a minute later the power went off with a bang; the music stopped and the whole place was cast into darkness. Bruce and Andy ran for their lives.

Margie had been dancing cheek-to-cheek with Hugo on the dance floor and, not knowing the layout of the place, yearned for a bit of privacy where they could be more intimate without being embarrassing. And then - alleluia – out went the lights!

Hugo took her arm and led her over to an alcove where there was no other form of life and, in the darkness so conveniently caused by her jealous boyfriend, they got down to some serious business on the sofa.

This was the moment that changed Margie's life; Hugo was so gentle, so loving and yet so strong that she could never go back to what she now knew was only "second best" with her surfer boyfriend or, to be more accurate, "ex-boyfriend".

Bruce for his part was also engaged in a life changing phenomenon for, as he raced across the dark space in front of the surf club, he tripped on a metal bar that was sticking out from the wall and fell hard down on to the concrete path in such a way as to break the femur in his upper right leg. He was howling in pain and could not move. Andy tried to pick him up so as to get away from the scene of the crime but that only exacerbated the pain. Footsteps could be heard coming down the stairs as the clubbies wanted to know why they had suddenly been deprived of light and sound.

Andy heard them and, not having much moral fibre in his make-up, he ran away like a coward in the night, leaving his wounded friend to be captured by the troops of the enemy.

The lifesavers arrived with torches and it didn't take them long to find the groaning man. Then one of them went over to his car and noticed that its tyres had been let down.

"Should we ring the ambulance or the police first?" asked one of the clubbies.

"Ambulance," replied the club captain. "He won't be going anywhere fast; there'll be plenty of time for the cops later. Fingerprints should solve everything. It's one of them surfers; at least that's one less of the little rats to defy us in the water by surfing where we tell them not to."

While all this was going on downstairs another drama was taking place in the dark alcove of the social room. With the power off for the night there was plenty of time for Margie and Hugo to get to know each other more intimately and both of them expressed their gratitude to the kind god who had given them pitch darkness at the very moment when their passions demanded it.

When the case came to court Bruce hobbled in and pleaded guilty as the fingerprint evidence was overwhelming. "And what was the cause of the grievance that gave rise to all this wanton vandalism?" asked the magistrate, a crusty old misogynist who never went to the beach.

"A woman, your worship," replied the prosecutor.

"A woman! It's always a bloody woman."

"Yes, your worship. Apparently there is a lot of bad blood between the surfboard riders and the lifesavers. Each group seems to think that they own the beach to the exclusion of the other. And this girl, who had been going out with a surfer, crossed the line and joined the lifesavers without getting a release from the surfing group."

"Sounds like the English football league," said the magistrate. "Transfer fees and all that. Surely the beach is big enough for everybody." He then sentenced Bruce to two years' probation and a fine of $10,000.

"Well, you really are quite a gal," said Hugo as he walked hand in hand with Margie along the water's edge just as the sun was setting.

"What do you mean?"

"Now that we are to all intents and purposes a "pair" you must be the only girl in Mussel Bay to have been the girlfriend of both a surfer and a clubbie."

"Why not?" she replied. "Surely the beach is big enough for everybody."

WAVEBAND

"Hello, this is William Wavenut from Surf Radio reporting from Ocean Beach. After we've given the surf report, the latest contest results from around the world and our surf quote for the day we shall move on to our one hour programme of surf music and then our talkback topic for the day which poses the question of whether surfing is a religion, an addiction or a social problem."

Fast forward to the Talkback Show....

"I would like our first caller to be someone who is still wet from surfing. Do we have any such creatures or have they all been towelled dry by their lovely girl-friends on the beach? Yes. I hear a ring. Hello."

"Hi, I'm Jay. I've just come in from a surf and I'm up at my car eating a mango."

"Do you still have the salt water dripping from your hair?"

"Yes, and it's now pouring down through my nostrils as well."

"Right, so you're a genuine waverider just out of the briny. The perfect specimen to start off our discussion. So, Jay, what is it? A religion, an addiction or a social problem?"

"For me it's an addiction. I am a wave addict. Whenever I see a wave I have this overpowering urge to ride it. I just have to have every wave."

"So, you drop in on others?"

"All the time. I just have to because I'm an addict."

"Well, I'm glad I don't surf at your beach. I reckon I'm a pretty generous sort of guy but when I go to all the trouble of driving to the beach, squeezing into a wettie and then paddling out through the cold sea I wouldn't want to give up my waves to an addict like you. Have you ever sought treatment for your addiction from a waves counsellor?"

"No."

"Why not?"

"Because they're too much like drugs counsellors. Always trying to stop people enjoying themselves. Real killjoys. Not my type at all. 'Just Say No' and all that crap; I'm a 'Just Say Yes' man."

"You're a wise addict, Jay. Pleasure for pleasure's sake and all that. You and I must hear the beat of the same drum."

"Yes, I think I must be an addict by nature. Do you think I've chosen the right addiction?"

"Yes, but it could be dangerous."

"How?"

"All that dropping in on other surfers. Had any punches in the nose?"

"No, because I've got a magic surfboard and everybody in the bay knows it."

"So?"

"One day when I dropped in on someone he came up to me on the beach and was going to punch me in front of all the crew."

"So what did you do?"

"I told him that I was an addict and that my surfboard had supernatural powers. I then touched the top of his head with the nose of my board and he fell down in an epileptic fit. Now they just let me drop in on them because they know I'm an addict with strange powers."

38

"Yes, but you don't have any powers over your addiction, do you?"

"No, and I don't want to. Listen, mate, I've been talking to you long enough and I'm starting to feel withdrawal symptoms. I just have to get back into the waves for another fix."

"Good on you, Jay, and just keep away from those waves counsellors. Next caller…"

"Good morning, William. I'm Nick and I can fully understand where the last caller is coming from because I'm an ex-wave addict and I know what it's like."

"What do you mean – an 'ex-wave addict'? Does that mean you no longer surf?"

"No, I just turned my addiction into a religion. The waves are now my God instead of my master. Jesus was the first surfer and we are all His followers. When He walked on the Sea of Galilee that was the beginning of surfing. And all surfers are His disciples. That's why it's a religion. But I only found that out after being an addict. You see, addiction usually leads to religion."

"All right, so we have a score of one all. What about the third option? Is anybody prepared to say that surfing is a social problem?"

"Hi, William, My name's Susie and I agree with your first caller that surfing is an addiction."

"And is it an addiction for you?"

"Well, sort of – except I've never been on a surfboard."

"Hey, Susie, are you on Planet Earth?"

"I'm on the edge. Most addicts are on the edge. I am not so much addicted to surfing as to surfers. Ahhh! I'm starting to feel all gooey. Whenever I see a tanned

39

hunk walking down the beach with his surfboard under his arm all I want to do is rip his board shorts off his tight little bum and get him in the pit."

"Susie! This is a public programme. There might be some nuns listening."

"I can't help it. I just want all the surfers to know how I feel. My phone number is 349-6537 and I'm available twenty-four hours a day. I can handle more than one at a time. The whole beach if necessary." Click.

"Well, that sounds like a real addict. Did you get that, boys? Telephone number 349-6537. I repeat 349-6537. We shall repeat this number again at the end of the programme and then at five minute intervals throughout the day and night. Next caller."

"Hello, Mister Wingnut."

"My name's Wavenut."

"Very well, Mister Wavenut. I beg to differ from the last nut and the nut before. In fact, I'd get more sense out of a macadamia nut."

"Do you have an addiction to nuts?"

"No, and if you speak to me like that, I'll come round to your radio station and kick you in the nuts."

"You seem a very polite gentleman and my powers of intuition tell me that you're going to say that surfing is a social problem."

"It's more a medical problem. The main reason that surfers spend all summer in the waves is to increase the skin cancer statistics. They should protect themselves by surfing with umbrellas."

"Oh dear, another killjoy – this time from the 'health scare' department. Don't you know that the sun gives us health and vitality? It's also a nice feeling to lie in the sun; that's why we're told not to do it. Next caller."

"Hi, dude, I'm Jude. I would have to say that for me surfing is a religion. I get up early for the dawn session just like Catholics get up for Mass. I take my place in the line-up just like they take their place in the pew. When I am out there in communion with the waves it is an intensely religious experience. I feel very close to nature and to God. And God obviously appreciates my presence in His ocean because he gives me some really good waves to ride. That's all, amen."

"Thank-you, Jude, and next time you're out there, ride one for me. Do we have any more addicts as they seem to be the most interesting callers?"

"Yes, I'm Charlie. Well, that's not my real name but my friends call me Charlie. When I see the powdery white foam of the breaking wave I just can't help myself. It gives me such a buzz. I just have to ride it and then paddle out and do it again. I seem to have a nose for that sort of thing. Does that make me an addict?"

"Well, yes, but it's also quite normal."

"But I don't want to be normal."

"Then don't be. And because of your subtle and witty contribution to the programme I am going to award you the prize of the day. A box of tissues for runny noses. So you can now get out there and be a real Charlie. Do we have any other callers?"

"Yes, good morning Mister Wavebat. My name is Mrs. Clifford and I'm seventy-five years old next birthday and on my bathroom scales I weigh nine stone, eight without my clothes on. I say that surfing is a social problem."

"Why?"

"Because I live next door to a house full of surfers and they have rowdy parties all night."

"So why is that a social problem?"

"You see, it's a social gathering and they don't invite me. That's why for me it's a social problem."

"I suggest, Mrs. Clifford, that next time you get on your bathroom scales you then go straight over next door and present yourself at the party in your birthday suit. That might solve your problem. Next caller."

"My name is James and until I started listening in to your programme this morning I would have classed myself as a surf addict but now I think I'm a telephone addict."

"Why?"

"I've been dialling 349-6357 for the last twenty minutes but it's always engaged. If that broad's always on the phone, how does she have the time for the other thing?"

"She probably does it with the receiver in her ear."

"Hello. Is that William Wavenut?"

"The man himself."

"I am Mizzz Beasley, the chief executive of the Commission for turning the Recalcitrant Human into the Good Citizen."

"So you're the Thought Controller?"

"Oh, we never use that term."

"So what's your gripe?"

"How do you know what I'm thinking?"

"Well, with a job title like that you wouldn't be ringing up Surf Radio Talkback unless you did have a gripe. So, surfing is a social problem, is it?"

"Not *a* social problem. Many social problems. Do you want me to list them?"

"So long as it doesn't take more than half an hour."

"First, head injuries in the water when a surfer gets hit on the head by his board. This is adding to health costs.

Secondly, when the surf is up some schools find that half their male pupils are out in the waves instead of in the classroom.

Thirdly, the waves are an uncontrolled and anarchic environment beyond the reach of normal, land based law enforcement agencies. It is not in the interests of society in general to have any group outside the control of the authorities. People need to be watched over for their own good.

Fourthly, too many surfers take illegal drugs which creates all sorts of problems for our poor, overworked counsellors.

Fifthly, there have been complaints of wild, all night surfers' parties which causes noise pollution.

Sixthly, the surfing scene seems to attract impressionable teenage girls who hardly wear any clothes on the beach, thereby exposing themselves to the risk of sexual abuse.

Seventhly,..."

"Oh, shut up, you silly old cow. What you're really trying to say is that you don't want either surfers or their girlfriends to have any fun. You want us all to be as miserable as you and all your sexually frustrated colleagues. If you could open your eyes and look beyond your narrow tunnel vision you would see that your lot, with your itch to dictate to others how to live their lives, are the real problem in society. You're just a sad bunch of killjoys who need to get a life." Click. "Phew! I desperately need a call from an addict to restore my faith in the human race. Any more addicts out there?"

"Yes, I'm Roly and I'm an addict. I'm addicted to anything that I really like. In fact, I just can't get enough of good things."

"Like surfing?"

"Yes, and jelly beans. I like the red ones best."

"Why?"

"Because I've got a red surfboard and I like to be colour co-ordinated. I also have red board shorts. And red hair."

"So you must look like a map of the British Empire?"

"Yes, and geography is my favourite subject."

"My word, you do sound like a well co-ordinated addict. But tell me, Roly, why are you addicted to surfing and red jelly beans?"

"Because they both make me feel good."

"'Feel good'. Two great words to wind up this discussion on the nature of surfing. From the wide variety of calls it is quite obvious that surfing is both an addiction and a religion. There have been a few callers who have declared it a social problem but, since they don't surf, they don't count and by now they have probably died of their worries anyway.

And now I must hand you over to sweet Shelley who is going to talk about the latest fashions in bikinis for the next hour and a half while I go surfing. She will be talking all about floral bikinis, striped bikinis, shrink wrap bikinis, draw string bikinis, polka dot bikinis, see-through bikinis, leopard skin bikinis, fishnet bikinis, disposable bikinis, edible bikinis and all the other teenie weenies that we like to see worn on the beach. And all you randy surfers out there – don't forget Susie's number. 349-6537. See ya."

SEEING DOUBLE

Tom and Tim Bevan were identical twins. Same height, same weight, same shape, same voice, same face and same long, shaggy, blond hair. There were only really two differences between them: Tim was right handed whereas Tom was left handed and Tim was one of the best surfers in the world while Tom wasn't. They were both natural footers who took part in contests up and down the Californian coast but, while Tim often found himself in the Final, Tom was invariably a first or second round loser. It was not as if Tom was a "rabbit" but he just wasn't as good as Tim – especially in the bigger waves.

The brothers were exceptionally close and when Tim won a place in the Top 44 and scored a six figure sponsorship deal, his only real regret was that he would be away from Tom for much of the year on circuit. However, Tom was gracious about it and said that he was just as pleased to stay at home, surfing Ventura Beach with all their friends.

The pro tour was in three parts and Tim was able to return home for a month's break between the various sectors.

In the first three contests he did surprisingly well for a newcomer and finished up in fourth position with not many points separating Numbers One to Four. Not surprisingly, his sponsor, Sammy Stevens of the Stevens Surf Company, was delighted. He reckoned that he had got one of the world's best surfers for a price that was way below what other sponsors had paid for Numbers One, Two and Three.

Having been in the spotlight while on tour with cameras clicking in front of him both in the waves and on the dance floor afterwards, Tim was very particular about his privacy when he returned home. He had done his bit for his sponsor on tour and now he just wanted to be left alone for a month to get some good waves with his brother and their friends and to hang loose in the evenings in his own way.

The problem was that on one of these evenings he went to a twenty-first birthday party where he met a spunky young lady with whom he fell instantly and madly in love. This was less than a week before he was to rejoin the circuit for the second leg of the pro tour in Europe.

Jessie was a student nurse and, as mad as she was on Tim, she just could not abandon her course to travel with him on tour while he for his part could not bear to be separated from her for the three months of contests that constituted the important second leg of the tour. Nor could he pull out as that would be a breach of the contract that he had signed with his sponsor – a contract that was worth more than a quarter of a million dollars. Nor would Sammy Stevens release him voluntarily for he believed that he had a budding world champion on his hands.

As the day of departure approached Tim became more and more agitated and, as always, he confided in his younger brother (by six minutes).

They were sitting in the sand hills watching the sun set over the blue Pacific when Tim unloaded his heart to his "other half". Tom's initial offer was to take over Jessie "since she wouldn't know the difference and we've done it before" but Tim said that that was out of the question. Instead, he made a counter offer.

Because it was only a few days since he had met his lady love and nobody, apart from themselves and Jessie, really knew of it, why couldn't Tom take his place on tour so that he could stay home and develop what he claimed was the most important relationship of his life?

"But that would be fraud!" exclaimed Tom. "Defrauding both the sponsor and the surfing authorities. Years in jail for both of us if they found out."

"Yes, but nobody would ever know. Just you, me and Jessie."

"Sammy Stevens would go ballistic. You know how happy he is with your results."

"Yes, but I've never felt like this before. Don't you want to go on the circuit? Girls, parties and everyone putting you on a great fuss?"

"But I'm hardly likely to hold your position at Number Four."

"Yes, but it's such a strong position that we can afford to drop a few places."

By the time it was dark they had made their decision. Tom would fly out on Friday for the European sector of the tour while Tim would stay behind with Jessie. They both knew that it was daring, risky and probably foolhardy; in the event of being found out they would both be in the dock on a charge of fraud. A major felony.

In the hours before the departure Tim was frantically trying to remember and relate to Tom all the things that had happened on the first leg in case some of the other pros started talking about them and, of course, it was necessary to fill Tom in on all the conversations that had taken place between Sammy Stevens and his sponsored surfer.

Tom was nervous as he boarded the plane while his reckless brother was ecstatic as he held Jessie in his arms and looked forward to three months of loving bliss.

Tom was lucky that the first contest was held in waves no bigger than two and a half feet. This put everyone on an even footing and, with his graceful style, he found himself winning heat after heat until he was beaten in one of the two semi-finals. So far so good.

The next contest was a bit further down the coast and the waves were just as puny and pathetic. Again Tom reached the semi-final and, because of the unimpressive showing of Number Three, he found that "T.Bevan" had now moved up to Number Three position. The plan was working to perfection and Tom was proving to himself at least that in small wave contests the whole meaning of a "world championship" was utterly meaningless; it seemed that any half good surfer could win.

The next contest was also held in small surf and Tom was put out in the third round and so dropped back to Number Fourteen. And from then on it was all downhill.

The contest that began the following week was in bigger and more challenging waves and Tom found that he was outclassed by all the experienced pros. He should have been put out in the first round but the judges tended to judge him on T. Bevan's rising reputation rather than on T. Bevan's actual performance and so he received the benefit of the doubt. But when he put up an equally dismal showing in the next round they could carry him no longer and so he was a second round loser in the best waves of the sector so far. And that was not the end of his woes.

"Ah, Tim, can we have a quick word?" asked Sammy Stevens.

"Of course," replied Tom.

"Now, remember what you promised me just before the first contest at the beginning of the year – when we went for that long walk along Coconut Beach?"

"Yes," stammered Tom.

"What was it?"

A dead silence. "Well, I promised a lot of things but I don't know what exactly you're getting at," said Tom.

"You can't remember?"

"Well, not really."

"Are you on drugs or something? Is that why your performance is dropping?"

"No."

"Then it's a good thing that you're a surfer and not an intelligence agent. With a memory like that you wouldn't even remember whose side you're on." As they were parting Sammy grabbed him by the shoulder and said very seriously and very confidentially, "I don't want to see you a second round loser in next week's contest. You are to be where you belong and that is at least in the semi-finals. Got it?"

Tom knew that that depended on the waves and unfortunately there was another big swell that produced strong and difficult surf. But Tom did not repeat his performance of losing in the second round; instead he was put out in the first round. And he was now down to Number Thirty-five.

Back home Tim was having a ball. Unlike the small waves in Europe Ventura and Rivermouth had produced great surf virtually every day since his brother had left; Tim spent his days in the waves and his nights with Jessie. He had never been happier and when he heard that "T. Bevan" had fallen from Number 4 to Number 35 he was unfazed; people in love tend to have their own priorities.

Meanwhile the continuing fall of T. Bevan in the rankings was becoming a bit of a story as surf writers and administrators were posing the question "How could someone who made such a dashing start lose form so quickly?"

There were only two more contests to go; the first one was held in waves that were not much more than a ripple and Tom reached the quarter finals. But Huey really turned it on for the last contest and poor old Tom was again a first round loser. In fact, he didn't get a single good ride.

That night Sammy Stevens took him to dinner to discuss his erratic form as "I've invested a lot of money in you and I expect results".

They ate at a French restaurant called Le Chien Qui Rit – the Laughing Dog – and they both chuckled at such a striking name. While Sammy had a seafood dish Tom opted for the roast lamb. Sammy noticed that Tom was cutting the meat with a knife that he held in his left hand whereas the last time they had dined on the night that the sponsorship deal had been signed, he had cut the steak with his right hand.

The next morning Tom flew back home for the month long break between the second and third legs of the tour. Next stop: Hawaii.

"Well, little brother," asked Tim, "what's it like to be a pro on the circuit?"

"It has its ups and downs. How is the romance going?"

"Hot, intense and steamy. It was the best decision I ever made to stay back here. I've had the best few weeks of my life."

"Well, I haven't and there's no way I can do the Hawaiian sector. Sunset at twelve feet and all that."

"Funny you should say that because Jessie's got her holidays coming up and they just happen to coincide with the dates of the Hawaiian contests. Now that I've had a good rest I'm rarin' to go again and she can come to Hawaii with me. Would you like to pass the baton back to Tim?"

"Too right. I don't think my nerves could stand the strain much longer. I've been reading all the fraud cases in the paper and it seems that it's never less than twenty years behind bars. And, since we're both in it together, they'd probably throw a conspiracy charge in as well. We'd be old age pensioners by the time we got out."

The first contest of the final leg of the tour was at Pipeline and Tim, refreshed by his lengthy break from competitive surfing, came back with a vengeance and won the contest. This pushed him up to Number 12 and, of course, Sammy was delighted as he realised that Tim was back to the form that he showed at the beginning of the year.

The next week his star surfer shone again at Sunset and reached the semi-final. This put him at Number 7 and in the final contest, held at Waimea, he reached the final before losing to the World Champion. He therefore finished the season at Number 5.

Before going to the awards ceremony in Honolulu Tim had to have dinner with Sammy to discuss the year's results as well as future moves. Sammy opened the conversation by saying that, if Tim had kept his form during the latter part of the all-important second leg, he would now be World Champion. Tim nodded his head in agreement; after all, the figures proved it. He also knew how angry the sponsor would be if he knew the real reason for the drop in form.

Having surfed all the afternoon Tim was as hungry as a horse and so he ordered a prawn cocktail followed by roast beef that was served in two huge slices that covered most of the plate. Sammy noticed that he cut the meat with his right hand just as he did when they signed the sponsorship deal but not on the last occasion when they ate at the Laughing Dog.

"What was the name of that French restaurant where we last ate?" he asked Tim.

"I don't remember. Some French name, I think."

"And remember what we saw outside on the street afterwards when we were waiting for the taxi?"

Obviously something entertaining. "Yes, it was very funny," said Tim.

"You think it's funny to see all those ambulances rushing to an accident?"

"Oh yes, I've always laughed at ambulances. Something to do with when I was a child and I had a toy ambulance with a clown inside."

"Since you're ambidextrous I'd like you to switch the knife into your other hand and cut the meat that way. Like you did at the Laughing Dog."

"No, I do it in rotation according to the days of the week and on Sundays I use only my right hand. I don't want to get out of sync."

"You and your brother did a switch, didn't you?"

"What do you mean?"

"That's why your form dropped during the second leg? Because the 'T. Bevan' was Tom and not Tim?"

Oh, hell! This was worse than smallpox, SARS and a shark attack all at the same time."

"Just hypothetically, what would happen if we did?"

"What would happen? Everything would happen."

By now Sammy was panting like a dog as he seemed to be in a state of high excitement and great expectation. Instead of being furious at losing the prospect of sponsoring a world champion, he was positively beaming. It was as if there was a new force in the universe and all that Tim had to do was admit the truth in order to detonate the explosion. Since he was a thrill seeker he decided to go for it.

"Yes, we did a switch. I surfed the first leg, Tom did the second leg and I came back for the third."

"Why?"

"Because I fell in love with a local girl and wanted to stay with her when the second leg was on."

"Oh, my God! This is even better than what I thought."

"What do you mean? Aren't you angry at being deceived? If you like, I'll pay you back the sponsorship money."

"No, that won't be necessary. Can't you see what we've got on our hands? And to think that I was disappointed to think that you could have been World Champion! Anyone can sponsor a World Champion; after all, there's one every year and it's no longer very special. But what I'm sitting on is the greatest story ever to come out of competitive surfing – or competitive sport for that matter. Tim, my boy, you're worth your weight in gold. Of course, there'll be a Hollywood blockbuster about it and you and your brother will have to play the key roles. After all, where else would they find two identical twins who can surf? It's unique. You are freaks as well as celebrities. This is a real life drama like no other – fraud, daring, risk taking, being found out and then, to top it off, a love story as the dynamic force that set the whole thing going. Not even Shakespeare could have dreamt up this. If you and your brother agree to make me your agent, we'll all be set up for life."

A few days later Tim, Tom and Sammy sat at a table in a Los Angeles convention centre with dozens of microphones in front of them and hundreds of reporters. The story was run on every television channel which resulted in calls to talkback radio, letters to the editor and an endless topic of conversation. All over the planet the twins' photo and story was plastered across front pages and it seemed that the world just could not get enough of them. In Burma and Bulgaria, Turkey and Tasmania, and Washington and Warsaw they became household names while the World Champion was virtually unknown.

"What I don't understand," said Tim, "is that we did such a grotty thing and yet we are now more famous than any other surfer."

"That's what sponsorship is all about," replied Sammy. "It is all about publicity. The truth is that contest results simply don't matter."

A MATTER OF KARMA

Jack was not a happy lad. For one thing his surfboard was broken and he didn't have enough money to get it fixed. He had just flunked his exams at university and was staring into a future that was unknown and uncertain. How different it all looked when he had begun his course a couple of years earlier. For one thing he had then had a father, a family farm and a future but the rural downturn, coupled with the dishonest behaviour of the bank, had destroyed all three.

To tide him over the temporary slump in agricultural prices Jack's father had taken on an extra mortgage over the farm and then, being a couple of days late with a repayment, had everything stolen from under him by the bank which had verbally agreed to a late payment but had then gone back on its word. Result: a mortgagee sale of the farm and family home, both of which had been bought for a song by the adjacent owner who just happened to be the brother-in-law of the bank manager.

Devastated and humiliated, Jack's father had gone into the woods with a hand gun and shot himself through the head. Upon Jack's mother being told the news she had a heart attack and died five weeks later.

How Jack had ached to get away from it all by going on a surfing trip to some distant waves but there just wasn't enough money to pay for the fare. In fact, he did not even have sufficient in his account to pay the rent that was due on his one room flat.

All his life Jack had been a good and honest lad who had been through several phases of belief, one of which was the age old Eastern concept of karma. He had seen it work in small ways but, as a result of his string of recent misfortunes, he was beginning to have his doubts.

As he stood outside the bank waiting for it to open so that he could draw out the last fifty pounds in his account it started to rain. It was also bloody cold and his mind wandered yet again to the clear blue skies and perfect waves that he was always seeing in the travel articles of surf magazines.

He waited in the queue for the teller to check his balance as he could not even be sure that he had enough to cover a cheque for fifty pounds. When he finally reached the teller he noticed that it was someone he hadn't seen before – a young woman with a veil who could barely speak English. "Part of the cheap immigrant labour that banks now employ to replace the tens of thousands of better qualified staff that they have sacked in recent years", he reasoned.

The black clad woman tapped some buttons on her computer and began writing some figures on a piece of paper. Jack thought that it was taking longer than usual. She then handed him the slip of paper with his balance on. He looked down and saw the figure of £2,020,252-34. Without batting an eyelid he asked for a print-out showing all transactions since his last statement. She pressed a few more buttons and handed him a larger piece of paper. He read it and saw a credit entry of the previous day for £2,020,202 which, he realised, was a computer glitch of twos and zeros. It was marked "Refund of bank charges" so at least some other customer would not be losing out. Only the bank. Jack smiled, thanked the teller and walked over to the public desk to consider his options.

Jack had always been scrupulously honest in his dealings with others and would be the last person to cheat or deceive. That was his moral code but, he reflected, the bank had, by its dishonest behaviour, put itself outside the normal moral code. "Do unto others as they do to you", he whispered under his breath as he wrote a cheque for £4,000 cash and returned to the same teller.

Following the rigid and impersonal bank procedures she asked for his identification and he obliged by handing over his driving licence. A few minutes later he walked out of the bank with four grand in his bulging wallet. He went across the road to the coffee bar with thoughts of Bali and Hawaii pounding through his brain.

After ordering a strong black from the waitress he sat down to do some thinking. He knew that, even when they made mistakes, banks were legally in the right because, through overdrafts, they had the judges in their pockets. After all, a judge with a large overdraft was hardly likely to bite the hand that was feeding him. Therefore, Jack knew that he would never legally get away with it – at least not in Britain. But the world is a big place and, he reflected, there are many spots that are warmer and have better waves than dear old Blighty.

What he planned to do was risky but, he reasoned, risk-taking was part of the thrill of being a surfer. All surfers take risks when they paddle out in the big stuff. If a person was not a risk-taker, he would not go surfing. But the risk that Jack was about to take would be in a different category altogether. If he came unstuck, the consequences would be dire; if he pulled it off, he would be made for life.

He reckoned that he had no more than a day before the error might be picked up and so he caught a taxi to the next branch of the same bank where, after identifying himself to another rookie teller, he drew out a further £7,000.

By now there was no more room in his pockets for the money and he was fast becoming a worthwhile mugging target. It was now time for the big one so he went home, put on his best suit and rang up the telephone company to get the names and numbers of some Swiss banks.

He then returned to the nice teller who had given him the good news in the first place. He told her that the bulk of the account – exactly £2,000,000 was to be sent by telegraphic transfer to a bank in Switzerland and he gave her its name and address. He then filled out a form, signed it and handed it over to the teller together with his driving licence as well as his passport. She checked both the balance and the ID and, since everything was in order, effected the transfer.

Jack had now enriched himself by £2,011,000 which, he felt, was the karma for all the misery that the bank had inflicted on himself and his family in recent months.

Jack went home and found a note on his front door from the landlord, reminding him that his rent was overdue. He walked in, closed the door and burst out laughing. He extracted from his wallet a full month's rent and put it on the front table for the landlord to collect. Then, remembering how the old boy had looked after him on a few occasions when he had been late paying, he put another £200 in the envelope.

He then packed his belongings into a couple of bags, leaving his broken surfboard behind, and took a taxi to Heathrow. An hour and a half later he was on a flight to Zurich. First Class.

He knew that he could never return to Britain but, in view of what had happened to him in recent times, not to mention the grey skies and driving rain that the plane flew through as it gained height over Richmond, he decided that exile was a price that he was prepared to pay in return for a surfing holiday that would never end.

By the end of the day he had presented himself at the bank in Zurich which, happy to have a new customer of such substance, was very obliging in helping him to place the funds in a secret numbered account that would bear enough interest to give him an annual income of a little over £140,000 which, the bank told him, would be tax free so long as he never spent more than three months of any year in the same Western country. This was not a problem since the essence of a surfing holiday is that you keep moving on.

The next day he found one of Switzerland's few surf shops where he bought two new boards, a couple of wetsuits, three rash vests and a dozen pairs of board shorts. His new life had begun.

Bali was his first destination; the heat, colour and energy that hit him as he emerged from the terminal building at Denpasar Airport seemed like another world from the one he had left behind.

Jack rented a large, two storey bungalow with a thatched roof that was only a few yards from the waves of Legian beach. It had lots of little balconies and a large lawn where he could lie in the sun between surfs.

He rode the long waves that roll over Kuta Reef, he surfed right into the cave at Uluwatu but he found Padang Padang on a big day rather frightening. He also developed a genuine liking for the smiling and gentle Balinese people; he adopted not only their clothes, by wearing a sarong, but also some of their laid back attitudes to the world around them.

At night he became a party creature, moving effortlessly among the *beau monde* who have long been attracted to this most beautiful and romantic of islands like moths to a lamp.

After surfing and partying for six weeks he found that, thanks to the favourable exchange rate, he had spent only a fraction of his monthly allowance and so he decided to rectify the situation by throwing a party to end all parties on his 21st birthday which fell in a week's time.

When he asked Wayan, the owner of his bungalow, if it would be all right to have a party on the lawn, the smiling little man in the bright red sarong replied that, since Bali was an island of pleasure, what could be more natural than Jack inviting all his friends to share his birthday?

They then discussed the nuts and bolts of the operation but, when Jack said that some of the guests would get so hot in the warm tropical night that they would want to run down the beach and cool off in the sea, Wayan changed his smile from one of happiness to one of fear, the Balinese having a different smile for every emotion. He whispered to Jack that the demons who live in *pasih* (the sea) are at their strongest and most dangerous during the hours of darkness and, if any of the guests should venture into the spirits' oceanic home at such an unpropitious hour, they would almost certainly never be seen again.

Jack knew enough of Balinese ways to appreciate the problem but he was not happy at having an all night party at the hottest time of the year without providing some means of cooling off. He cast his eyes along the lawn towards the beach. On one side of the grass was an overgrown section where Wayan threw old tree branches and grass clippings. Pointing to it, Jack exclaimed how wonderful it would be if there was a swimming pool there where everyone could cool off at night without bothering the demons of the sea. Wayan's eyes lit up at the prospect but he then asked the rhetorical question of how a poor man like him could find the money to pay for such a wonderful thing.

"How long would it take to build?" asked a curious Jack.

Wayan was non-committal, saying that he had one friend who was a large contractor with several teams of labourers and another who made pipes and tiles. He then explained how the main water pipes passed only a few yards from the property. Almost as a joke Jack said that, if it could be built within a week, he would pay for it.

He expected Wayan to scoff at the suggestion as who could turn an overgrown piece of ground into a brand new swimming pool in a week? Why, in the West it would take at least a year to get all the right permits from the local council. Imagine his dismay when he heard the smiling Wayan say that, of course, it could be built in a week.

While Jack went in for his afternoon surf Wayan sent his houseboys out with messages to deliver to his contractor friend, his plumbing friend, his tiling friend and all the others who would be needed to make the dream come true.

When Jack walked up on to the lawn after a long session in the waves he saw a hive of activity ahead of him. Measurements were being taken, drawings were being made and materials were being costed by all the tradesmen. Shortly before sunset they came up with a price. Jack did a quick conversion to Swiss francs and told them that, if they could guarantee to have it finished by the end of the week, he would pay for it. One of the tradesmen was so pleased at this quick money making opportunity that he offered to leave his teenage daughter with Jack as security for completing the work on time.

So delighted was Wayan at the munificence and imagination of this Westerner whom the gods had sent to stay in the bungalow that he told Jack that he could stay there free of charge for a month a year for the rest of his life. The astute mind of the Balinese reasoned that, with the added amenity of a swimming pool, he would be able to double the rent on the bungalow for the other eleven months which would more than pay for the month that Jack could stay there as a non-paying guest.

When Jack got up the next day for an early morning surf he could see teams of workers already starting to dig the great hole – not with a mechanical digger but by pick and shovel, with most of the heavy work being done by tiny Balinese women.

They worked day and night (under floodlights) and by the end of the third day the hole was complete and so was the trench that was to bring the water from the town pipes to the pool.

Contemporaneous with concreting and tiling the pool and landscaping the surrounds were Jack's other preparations for the party – the food, the drink, the music and the guest list. Having been a nightly party animal since arriving on the island, he had met and socialised with people from all over the world and so the invitation list was cosmopolitan but with a heavy weighting of female beauty.

With coconut palms and banana trees all around, Jack decided to make the tropical foliage the theme of the party. This was to be Bali's first "garden" party; the guys were told to wear only leaves while the girls were to wear only flowers "and not too many of them".

On the day itself the party people of Bali were busy picking flowers and stripping trees of their finest foliage. Banana leaves were fashioned into imaginative costumes while others opted for just a single figleaf in the strategic position.

The swimming pool was filled for the first time shortly after sunset and within the hour what looked like a moving jungle began to file through the gate into the compound of Jack's bungalow – the young, the beautiful, the stylish and the reckless, with nobody wearing anything other than leaves and flowers.

The party lawn was lit only by the moonlight and small candles flickering in the bushes. Along one side was a long table on trestles that was loaded with rice dishes, fresh fruit and other delicacies of the island while the smiling Balinese barmen cruised the "forest" of people, filling their glasses and entering into the fun and beauty of the occasion.

Daniel, a happy techno DJ from Cologne, did the spinning to provide the right sort of music for this unique surfers' party. He too was dressed in a single banana leaf around his middle which, he claimed, was so comfortable that he was going to wear it on the plane back to Germany the next day.

As the night wore on and the guests retreated further from reality the demands of passion caused some to shed their leaves as if it was autumn. The swimming pool provided a welcome refuge from the tropical heat as well as an intimate meeting place for the unattached.

Jack spent most of the night with the lovely Carole, a fashion designer from Paris, who was dressed in four hibiscus flowers – one behind her ear, one on each breast, and one down below. In this magical and romantic setting he sincerely believed that she was the most beautiful and desirable creature he had ever seen. To have her in his arms made the whole party – and all the money he had spent on the swimming pool – worthwhile.

Jack grew so fond of surfing in the warm Indian Ocean that he did not want to leave it. Although he could afford to fly on to Australia or America or anywhere else he decided to buy a boat and sail south-west towards the bottom of Africa, surfing whatever waves might be breaking on the islands in between.

He looked at several Indonesian fishing vessels before choosing one that seemed sturdier than the others. He bought it and had it rigged for what he described as "an indefinite trans-oceanic voyage in search of waves and whatever".

Once the word got out Jack was inundated with offers to join the crew. He chose a couple of Australian surfers with experience of seamanship and, at the last minute, Carole. Ever since the party they had been seeing more and more of each other – on the beach, in the bars and, of course, in the new swimming pool where they cooled off in the noonday sun and frolicked in its waters under the stars at night.

Taking advantage of the south-east trade winds, they sailed in a direction that was more east than south, stopping off whenever they came to an island to check out its waves. Thus did they surf reefs, points and beaches, break bread with the natives and generally expand their mental and physical horizons.

During the languid, tropical days and the warm, sensuous nights the romance between Jack and Carole blossomed like an apple tree in spring. They lived for the moment and every day seemed better than the last. "This is a journey that I never want to end," declared Jack as the two of them kissed on the stern deck against a backdrop of the orange sunset casting its fiery glow over the tranquil ocean.

When they pulled into the next island it was time to do a few repairs to the boat and to replenish supplies. Accordingly they decided to stay for a month or two in order to rediscover their land legs, do some surfing and acquaint themselves with the islanders.

Upon landing they were taken to see the chief in his wooden hut on top of the hill. He extended the island's traditional hospitality and made several trips down to the shore to see how the refurbishing of the boat was going. Slowly.

The chief and the other islanders were impressed at the way that the Westerners could stand up on their surfboards as they rode across the waves that had been breaking on the shore for thousands of years but had never hitherto been utilised for such an eye catching purpose.

There was a small, grass air strip on the island which linked it with the Big Island but the air route was rarely used – mainly for medical emergencies when it was necessary to fly someone to the Big Island for treatment.

The chief, in fact, owned several islands but this was the only one that was inhabited. Jack and his friends made some short sailing trips to some of the other islands of the chieftaincy to check out the surf. Most were surrounded by coral reefs but there was one that had a reef on one side, which enclosed a lagoon, and a superb point break on the other side which produced a succession of powerful and nicely formed waves that were just waiting for someone to ride them.

Finding a narrow channel through the reef, they passed through it and dropped their anchor in the calm waters of the lagoon. After paddling their surfboards to the shore they carried them half a mile across the island to the other side. The middle of the island was quite high with thick foliage and a fresh water stream that ran down into the sea. Between the point break and the mouth of the stream was a mile long beach of dazzling white sand that was lined with casuarina trees. As they crossed the island they noticed other trees laden with berries and fruit. As Carole said above the squawks of the seagulls, "I think we have found paradise." This sentiment was echoed by the boys when they came in from their long and exhilarating surf, each one declaring that the wave was one of the cleanest and most powerful they had ever ridden.

As Jack got to know the chief better he came to learn of some of the island's problems. No school for the kids, no hospital, poor housing and only subsistence living. "I have got so much land – all these islands – but no money," said the chief with a shrug. "All the money from trade and abroad goes to the Big Island and they keep it for themselves."

"Well, that's a funny thing," thought Jack, "because I've got loads of money but no land."

A few days later, when he reckoned that he knew the chief well enough to trust him, Jack asked if he could buy the uninhabited island of paradise that he had discovered; the purchase price would be enough to build a school and hospital as well as a new jetty and repairs to the broken down access road to the jetty so that their produce could more easily be traded with the Big Island. Both the chief and Jack believed that they had got the deal of their lives – as indeed they had.

Jack felt like Columbus arriving in the New World when he sailed across to his new abode with Carole, his two crew mates and a team of native labourers. In true pioneer fashion they cut down some of the trees and made them into log cabins – a large meeting house with a thatched roof of palm leaves for them to gather in the evenings for music and partying and some small cabins for sleeping; these were sited on different parts of the island and, in the interests of privacy, were separated from each other by trees and space. Tracks were cut, vegetable gardens were planted and a water system was made from the stream.

Jack was both the owner and the sovereign of the island and, as such, was able to name it and decide its form of organisation or "government". The first part was easy; this island and its wave seemed to be unique on the planet and so he named it "Peerless". Being a sociable creature, Jack hoped that others of the surfing tribe would come and surf the break with him. It would be a surfers' paradise and he would be the island's kind, loving and benevolent master. If Israel could be a land for Jews and Pakistan a land for Moslems, this would be the first "statelet" in the world that would be run for surfers.

Jack could not be its king as, even though he was "on the run" from England, he was still a subject of Queen Elizabeth and one monarch can not be the subject of another. Nor would it be a republic as he had always thought that there was something rather vulgar and fraudulent about republics. No, Peerless would be a feudal state which would be ruled by Jack for the benefit of himself and all the other surfers who would come to ride its waves.

Back on the chief's island a new school and hospital were already being built with part of the money that Jack's bank, on his instructions, remitted from Switzerland. There was enough left over to pay for a teacher, a doctor and a nurse from the Big Island and a new air of optimism prevailed.

Jack sent word to some of the surfing mates he had met on Bali to come out and share the pleasures of the island, ride its wonderful waves and provide him with company. He chose people who were as adept at making music and fun as riding a surfboard.

70

They would fly into the Big Island and then take the day long ferry trip to the chief's island where Jack would meet them in his boat and take them to Peerless. They brought with them other friends, their ladies, surfboards, musical instruments and books which formed a growing library in the annex to the meeting house.

In lieu of rent the guys would help Jack by working in the large vegetable garden, feeding the chooks and doing other manual work while the girls would help with the cooking. There were no laws – just the universal application of natural honesty, good manners and sensitivity towards others which, if practised universally, would make laws unnecessary.

However, sometimes the influence of the modern world would rear its ugly head as people, who were so used to being told what to do and having their minds moulded by their own interfering governments, were unable to handle true freedom. In such cases Jack would take the necessary steps in order to preserve the special character and unique freedom of the island.

The first such instance took place one night in the meeting house. A girl-friend of one of the surfers who had arrived for a fortnight's holiday complained about people smoking within the confined space of the meeting house and ordered them to "butt out". Of course, nobody took any notice of her, reasoning that, if she didn't like it, she could go outside instead of demanding that everyone conform to her ideas. To make sure that she got the point, Jack produced a packet of Indonesian clove cigarettes and handed them around. Everyone lit up and a few minutes later the meeting house and all around it was alive with the most powerful aroma that smoke can produce.

The next day Jack suggested that she leave his island home on the grounds that it was not her type of place. And so back she went to the bossy, highly regulated, discontented and argumentative Western world where she belonged.

But people like her were the exceptions as Jack and Carole played "mine host" to surfers from different countries and different backgrounds. Among this cosmopolitan lot was Phil, a young American surfer who didn't smoke or drink with the others but was the best of company and the life of the party. A couple of nights before he was leaving Jack asked him what he did back in the States to which he replied that he was a church minister who had taken a three month "sabbatical" in order to get some much needed R and R.

That night as he lay in bed Jack was thinking of what forces must be involved in bringing a man of God to this far flung island. Why, it was only the week before that, for the first time, he and Carole had talked about starting a family so that they could bring up children in the freedom and beauty of their island paradise..

Thus it was that the next day Rev. Phil McKenzie of the Presbyterian Church of the United States conducted a wedding on the beach near the point break where he united in holy matrimony the island's master and the lady who had been with him ever since that mad party on Bali several years earlier.

During the "reception" at the meeting house later that night Jack took his new wife by the hand and led her outside for a kiss under the stars. From this high point he thought back to the scene at the bank in

England where he made the decision that was to change his life. Carole said that they were the luckiest people in the world and that so much good fortune could only be connected with karma. "You do believe in karma, don't you?" she asked.

"Yes," he said emphatically, "but sometimes you have to do a few things and take a few risks to jog it along."

DIRTY BUSINESS

Morton (known to everyone as "Mort") was both smart and streetwise but he was also rather lazy. That was why he had been unemployed for more than a year. He lived in a fairly grotty flat above the beach with three other surfers and two dogs and spent most of his time in the waves. The sea was never as clean as it should be but it took a floating turd to smear against the back of his hand to rouse his anger and convince him that something really should be done to make the ocean cleaner for all the surfers, swimmers, fishermen and others who use it.

The following week he called a meeting at the local surf club of all those who were interested in ridding the ocean of pollution and that, not surprisingly, was most of the town.

At the meeting Mort was both eloquent and passionate as he rued the ever deteriorating situation and described in lurid detail all the health problems that could accrue to surfers if the present state of affairs was allowed to continue.

At the end of the evening a committee was elected, with Mort at its head, and it was entrusted with nothing less than the important task of negotiating with and bringing pressure on the authorities to solve this terrible problem.

The first action of the new committee was to organise a street march where they all held placards and called out slogans as they marched along the main street to the office of the local water company that dumped the town's sewerage into the ocean every day of the year.

The press and television companies had been alerted with the result that Mort was able to look at his

74

picture on the front page of the local paper as well as on the television screen where he enunciated very clearly the problem of pollution and set out what he wanted done about it. Everyone agreed that he was the ideal "front man".

The movement spread like a bush fire up and down the coast and, such was the passion for cleaner seas, that it soon had more than ten thousand paid up members. Mort appeared on a nationally televised current affairs programme and he started visiting schools to explain the problem to the students, many of whom were or would become surfers.

Of course, he drew expenses from the organisation for his travelling and other costs but there was still plenty left in the kitty from all the subscriptions and so he started to draw an honorarium as well. This was increased three times over the next few months so that by the end of the year Mort was earning more than four times what he had been getting on the dole.

Nobody begrudged him his honorarium because he really did put his heart and soul into the effort of educating the public about the problem of dirt in the sea. He was on television more and more frequently and was soon on the speaking circuit at meetings of Rotary, Round Table, Probus and women's groups where he spread the message with zeal and conviction. This thing was getting traction and, with an election coming up in eighteen months time, the government realised that it would have to do something or, more accurately, be seen by the voters to be doing something since in the modern "social democratic", media obsessed state perception is more important than substance.

The government did not want to lose the support of young people on whose naivety and gullibility it depended for a sizeable number of votes. That was why fat, bald headed, middle-aged Members of Parliament turned up in the front seats at rock concerts and pretended to understand the music. And if all these angry young surfers thought that not enough was being done on the pollution front, they might switch their votes to the Opposition. So Mort and his growing organisation would have to be neutralised.

The first step was to infiltrate the organisation with some undercover Party investigators to test the waters and assess the character of Mort and the gullibility of the members.

A few months later these undercovers made their report to party headquarters in which they suggested that Mort's Achilles heel was his desire to be in the limelight by giving speeches and appearing on television. It was felt that, if he could be made to feel important in the corridors of power, then he should be both "pliable and purchasable".

This report went right to the top – to the Prime Minister himself – who called in the Minister of the Environment to plot the strategy. "Of course, they've got a valid point and one that seems to go down very well with the voting public but the fact remains that we don't have the money to build all these new sewerage systems and anyway the water companies and the other industrial polluters are heavy contributors to party funds. And the first rule in politics is never to bite the hand that is feeding you.

So, if we can't confront these wretched surfers, we'll have to marginalise them and lock their growing movement into the endless process of meetings, reports and commissions. Our intelligence reports state that this Mort character – like most protest leaders – is a little nobody who is trying to be a big somebody. We'll make him a somebody all right. We'll kill him with kindness."

"You mean accede to their demands?"

"Of course not. As I said, we can't do that. No, we'll pull him on side and hold out the prospect of selecting him as one of our party's M.P.s. That way he won't give us any trouble. We will be controlling the movement through him and, because he is so blinded by the limelight and appearing on television, he won't realise how he is being used. So, Minister, those are the general guidelines and I'll leave the details in your competent hands."

Thus it was that the Minister, wearing a blue tie to match the ocean, stood on the main beach with the waves in the background to make a carefully orchestrated television announcement to the nation that a Commission would be set up to inquire into the problem of marine pollution and that it would conduct hearings and make its report within two years. This, of course, would be after the next election so that, if anyone questioned the government's commitment to cleaner seas during the election campaign, there would be a plausible and ready made answer. "There is a Commission sitting at present which is due to report very soon and the government will treat its recommendations with the greatest consideration."

In order to be doubly certain of getting the votes of Mort and all his members (now more than a hundred thousand) and indeed of all surfers, it was announced that Mort – as the representative of "a large organisation that deserves to have its voice heard" – would be a member of the Commission. Other Commissioners were the head of a water company, a tanker captain "to represent the marine industry" and several bureaucrats from the Department of the Environment. Each Commissioner would be paid for the two years of the Inquiry at a rate that for Mort was sixteen times what he had been getting on the dole. And sitting at a table in a committee room listening to others was certainly easier than being a brickie's labourer, which was the last job that he had.

From time to time the Minister would ring him up and ask his advice on this and that and a flattered Mort really believed that he had "arrived". He bought new suits and ties, cut his hair and even started to talk like a bureaucrat. And, of course, with his new found wealth he moved out of the grotty flat and bought a nice big house just across the road from the beach.

He no longer had much time for surfing as he believed that he had been "called" to a higher vocation – nothing less than representing the surfers in the important task of ridding the ocean of pollution. Power, respect and kudos.

The only problem was that turds were still floating about in the sea and surfers were getting mightily sick of it. Some of them broached the matter with Mort at public meetings of the organisation which, despite his busy schedule, he still attended – mainly because he always liked the applause that everyone gave him at the end for being "the public face of surfers in this vital task".

When some of these cheeky young brats stood up and told him that the problem was only getting worse, he felt defensive and, in order to justify the huge income that he was now receiving as a surfing environmentalist, he would stand up, give his trademark smile and declare that "important steps are currently under way with the Commission and it would be counter-productive to rock the boat at this particular juncture".

"Yes, but the turds are getting worse. Not to mention the condoms."

"You must understand that the process is ongoing and we should see some very positive results in the near future. Rome was not built in a day." Like all power trippers, he knew the importance of keeping the whole field to himself and making sure that no alternative voices made themselves heard. If anybody wanted an improvement in the state of the ocean, it could only be through Mort and his organisation. Nobody else must be allowed to queer the pitch.

In order to make sure that Mort would not "rock the boat" by refusing to agree with the other commissioners the Minister called him into his office at Parliament one evening for a drink. Mort now spent more time in Parliament than he did in the waves. That's because he was now so important.

"Ah, Mort, thank-you for coming," said the Minister by way of greeting. "I know how valuable your time is with the Commission and all your other worthy activities to keep our beautiful ocean free of pollutants. Now, there's an election coming up and our Party wants the surfers' vote and we don't want anyone rocking the boat. I'm sure that you must know by now that my Party is more committed to the environmental cause than the other lot. Therefore, if you can do your best to persuade your hundred thousand members to cast their votes our way, then you should see some movement towards something positive on the anti-pollution front within the life of the next parliament. Oh, by the way, this will be Mr. Derrington's last election. He will be retiring before the next one. You live in his electorate, don't you?"

"That's right."

"Well, as you no doubt know, it is important for political parties to plan well ahead and the Prime Minister has asked me if I have any ideas on a replacement for dear old Derro. As you know it is a safe seat for our Party and the one who is selected will be a certainty for a seat in the House. I told him that, if Mort proves reliable over the next year or two, the seat would be yours for the asking."

Mort was unable to conceal his delight as he thought of the big salary that M.P.s receive (far more than he was getting as a Commissioner), their excessive perks and the importance that the television companies and the public insist on giving them.

The next day the Minister reported to the P.M. "Well, how did it go?" asked the sweating leader. "Do we have him and his organisation in the bag? I've always believed that it is better to have those types inside the tent pissing out than outside the tent pissing in."

"I've made him think that he's going to be the next Member of Parliament for Weehampton-on-Sea for the election after this one."

"And he took the bait?"

"Of course."

"Then we shouldn't have any trouble with his organisation. Phew! That was a close one."

"Why?"

"Because cleaner seas is the one issue that we can't fight against. On most issues there are two points of view but not on that one. Who on earth could argue against cleaning up the oceans? That's why he and his lot were so potentially dangerous. But not any longer."

As expected, Mort proved very pliable His ego was now bigger than his passion for a cleaner ocean. Instead of railing against the authorities for not doing enough to clean up the seas he was now locked into the system of committees and endless meetings where all sorts of hot air was exhaled but nothing was ever done. But Mort believed that soon he would be an M.P. and then, no doubt, a minister. With such prospects in sight he convinced himself that it was not in the interests of either him or his movement to "rock the boat".

He also managed to convince most of the members of his movement not to embarrass the government as that would be "counter-productive in the circumstances". But not all surfers were prepared to sit back and wait while their leader went from one well-paid job to another. That was why Mort was now spending most of his time trying to keep the lid on protest as he sought to persuade the "hotheads" (just like he once was) to keep their powder dry and "listen to those of us who know how the wheels of power operate".

The only problem was that, despite all these committees, speeches, reports and television appearances, the pollution of the ocean was going from bad to worse. But Mort was now earning far more than most surfers, he was becoming a familiar sight on the television screens and he was rubbing shoulders with the powerful. And for him that was all that really mattered.

THE FIRST PRIZE IN LIFE

Eighteen year old Anton Oosthuizen was from an old Cape Dutch family who had arrived at the bottom of Africa at the beginning of the eighteenth century. Over the years they had played their part in the development of South Africa, raising cattle, growing grapes and even from time to time sitting in Parliament in Cape Town.

Anton's father was a successful and worldly wise lawyer who had studied common law at Cambridge and Roman-Dutch law at the University of Amsterdam. Although Anton had got good marks at school they would have been even better if he had not spent so much time in the ocean.

Living near the beach at Sea Point, he had first stood up on a surf board at the age of seven and, in the balmy climate and abundant waves of Cape Town, there were not many days since then that he had not donned boardies or wetsuit to ride what he could. His sporting and social life revolved around his local beach and his only real friends were his fellow surfers.

When he finished secondary school he expected to go on to the local university to study law. That would mean five years of hard slog but at least the campus was not too far from his favourite surfing spots and he would not be cut off from his friends.

His last ever day at school was Prizegiving Day and Anton was called up to the dais twice – school surfing champion and deputy dux. Not a bad mix!

That night Anton and his friends celebrated their formal transition from schoolboys into men with an orgy of smoking, drinking and partying at the surf club and it was with a very sore head that he woke up the next morning to put on his suit and tie and go into the city to have lunch with his father at the Pioneers' Club. The old man had said that he wanted to treat Anton to lunch for doing so well at the prizegiving and anyway, wasn't lunch at a gentleman's club all part of that transition to manhood – like when the boy in ancient Rome was given the *toga virilis*?

After they finished their steaks Mr. Oosthuizen led Anton into the Smoking Room where he ordered some coffee and handed Anton a cigar. A few minutes later, through the haze of cigar smoke, Anton told his father that he wanted to enrol at the University of Cape Town at the end of the summer holidays. "No, I've arranged something else," said Mr. Oosthuizen who had an irritating habit of always being right.

"Why?"

"Because, since the wonderful advent of 'majority rule' and its handmaiden, 'positive discrimination', our universities have been swamped with black students who are being admitted on the basis of their skin colour rather than their ability. Several of the professors are members of this club and they say that academic standards have plummeted since 1994 as learning and free thought are being replaced by the limited thinking of political correctness. And, since I had a first class education, I feel it my duty to see that you get the same. You live only once and I want you to be able to say that you won the first prize in life."

"I already have by being able to surf."

"There's more to life than surfing. I've made use of a few contacts and have managed to secure a place for you at my old university."

"Cambridge!" exclaimed Anton as he reflected on the magic of the word. "And week-ends surfing in Cornwall."

"No, your marks are not good enough for Cambridge but the University of Amsterdam has agreed to give you a place in their law school."

"No way. Holland doesn't have any decent waves. The British Isles block the powerful Atlantic swells. I'm not going there."

"So you will aim only for the second prize here in Cape Town?"

This struck a raw nerve in a young man of more than average ambition who was just starting out on his career. "I'll think about it," he drawled.

He did. And every time those words "the first prize in life" came spinning into his head. Did he really have the first prize in life or was it waiting for him over the horizon? Then that phrase "over the horizon" started to torment his increasingly confused mind for wasn't that what surfers were seeking all the time? An even better wave over the horizon? And as with surfing, so with life. Isn't that what inspired Columbus to cross the Atlantic and Bartholomew Diaz to discover the Cape? And old Piet Oosthuizen to leave crowded Holland all those years ago and give his descendants the privilege of living and prospering in the space and sunshine of South Africa? Yes, he agreed, there was more in life than surfing; that was why he had studied so hard at school. But to spend five years in a country which, by every law of geography, would be "surfless" was a big ask.

It was all too much for an eighteen year old just out of school so, having acquainted the rest of the surf club with his dilemma and finding them evenly divided in opinion, he gathered four of them as witnesses and tossed a coin in the air. As it rose towards the ceiling he called out, "Heads I go; tails I stay." It came down Heads.

The heavily suntanned, blond haired young man who arrived at Schipol Airport was stepping not only on to a new continent but into a new life. His luggage consisted of two bags of clothes and books as well as a couple of surfboards which he anticipated using on one or two long week-ends on the south-west coast of France.

He caught a train from the airport to Amsterdam Central Station. Every face on the train was strange and he was already missing his mates from the surf club. "Is this really the first prize or is it going to turn out to be the booby prize?" he wondered as the train sped through the flat countryside interspersed with canals, stone houses and the occasional windmill.

After leaving the station he checked into a small hotel just off Dam Rak that had bedrooms up its narrow staircase and a dimly lit but very lively coffee shop on the ground floor. He had a week before classes commenced and he intended to make the most of it.

After depositing his gear in his room a wide-eyed Anton went down to explore the ground floor. As he made his way to the counter to make a purchase he was accosted by a couple of young Dutch guys who, having seen him carrying his surfboards upstairs, asked him where he was from.

"Cape Town," he replied.

"And you have come to Holland to do some surfing?"

"Hardly; I don't think there are any waves here," replied Anton.

"Ha, ha. That's what we like everybody to think," said Johan. "That way we keep the waves free of crowds. All the surfing college kids who come over from America are here for the coffee shops and not the waves. But for those of us who live in Holland and know the scene we can enjoy both. If you like, I'll take you down to Scheveningen. I was down there this morning and the waves were about four feet and offshore."

"Where is it?"

"It's the beach for The Hague. That's our dreamy little capital. Full of bureaucrats and Eurocrats but fortunately they never come to the beach. It's less than an hour by car from here. Don't forget, Holland is very small and no place is very far. And no mountains to cross. Just fast, straight roads."

By now Anton had joined their table in the smoke filled room and it turned out that Johan and his friends, apart from being keen surfers, were also students at the university. In this new and strange city Anton was more than happy to have some congenial company while for their part they were happy to introduce a newcomer from South Africa to the delights of their gentle and ancient city.

After an hour they emerged from the coffee shop into the bright light of the late afternoon and made their way through the streets – filled with a young and fashionable crowd – to the Rembrandt Plein for a drink and a *tosti*.

From an outdoor table in the open square Anton watched the world go by – some of it very beautiful and interesting. They then walked along the tree-lined Heren

Gracht canal, the architecture of the gabled houses reminding him of the Cape Dutch buildings that grace the bottom of Africa.

They stopped at another coffee shop, which overlooked yet another a canal, and sat at an open window to roll a few. The night was warm and still and Anton, feeling more mellow by the minute, felt very comfortable with his new friends.

They then went for a walk in the red light district where every shape and size of the female form seemed to be on display – from matchstick size models to ones that resembled the baby elephants that he had seen in the Kruger National Park.

"But why are the ugliest ones the busiest?" he asked.

"Oh, come on, man, it's just your twisted brain. You stayed too long at the coffee shop. Haven't you heard of 'Beauty in the eye of the beholder'?" It was all very confusing.

They met up with an American college student from the University of Tennessee. When he learned that it was Anton's first night in Amsterdam and that he was to be a student at the University the college kid grabbed Anton's hand and shook it, exclaiming, "Congratulations, you have just won first prize in the lottery of life."

"What do you mean?"

"Listen, kid, I've sussed that place out. The university library on Spui has got a coffee shop across the road, a magic mushroom shop three blocks away and the red light district three blocks in the other direction. What more could a man want?"

"Waves," said Anton.

"Yes, and they're an hour away," put in Johan.

Shortly after midnight a terrible tiredness came over Anton and it was then that he realised that it had been more than forty-eight hours since he had slept. He had gone for one last surf at Clifton for three hours with his mates before catching the plane from the bottom of Africa to the north of Europe followed by his voyage of discovery around Amsterdam.

The others were going on to a late night bar but they told him how to get back to his hotel which was only a few blocks away. As he walked through the dark streets on his own he realised how far he was from Cape Town where such an exercise would almost certainly result in at least one mugging, if not more.

From the tourist boat mooring on Dam Rak he looked across the water at the floodlit station which, with its quaint gables and towers, appeared like something out of a fairy tale. "I think I'm going to like this place," he said to himself.

The next morning he met Johan and the others who drove him down to Scheveningen for his first taste of Dutch waves. They were much better than what he expected although not exactly Jeffrey's Bay.

After putting on their wetsuits the two surfers paddled out to the line-up and then along it as Johan introduced Anton to the other boardriders, each of whom shook hands with him and welcomed him to the wave. Then a big set came through and the others held back, calling out to Anton that the first wave belonged to him since he was the guest. He rode it hard and well and they all hooted.

Anton found the ambience of the line-up quite different from the "dog eat dog" attitude that was

88

becoming prevalent in the crowded waves of Cape Town. Holland might not have the best waves in the world but it certainly had the most friendly waveriders who seemed to get more fun out of their smaller surf than others get from bigger stuff.

Anton surfed with them every day until classes began. During that first magical week he quickly learned that the Dutch knew how to work hard and play hard.

On his first week-end he was taken to a clearing in the Ardennes forest where a "techno fest" was taking place. This was a two week long, non-stop rave for serious 24/7 party people. Anton and his friends dropped in for only one night and danced till dawn. He had first heard of this great wooded area during his Second World War history classes in South Africa and he half expected to see Hitler's Panzer divisions ramming their tanks through the trees on their way to invade Holland, Belgium and Luxembourg. But all was love, peace and gentleness in the forest to-night as happy partygoers were able to enjoy the multi dimensional pleasures of a rave under the stars and in a world of their own.

Too alert to sleep the next day (and night!), Anton cruised around Amsterdam with some of his new friends. Shortly after 4 a.m. one of them, Crazy Kobus, asked him if he would like to go for an early morning surf at Wijk aan zee.

"Why not?"

"You go and get your board and I'll go and get the transport. Meet you at the bridge across the road in half an hour."

"Roger."

"Who's he?"

"It's what we say for 'all right'."

Half an hour later Anton was standing on the bridge with his surfboard under his arm and his wetsuit hanging over it. He was looking down the road alongside the canal for Kobus when he heard a speedboat racing through the water. It slowed down and pulled up under the bridge. He looked down and saw Kobus at the wheel of a snappy little motor boat that was about eighteen feet long.

"Jump in, Anton. The best time for a cruise on the canals – just as the night is starting to fade and there's no traffic so we can go as fast as we like. I know the canal system like the back of my hand. I'll take you through to the North Sea Canal which leads down to the coast at Wijk aan zee."

He turned on the throttle and they were away – racing along the water past silent houseboats and under the arches of narrow bridges. Sometimes they went through water tunnels and came out the other side. With the sleeping city all around them they sped on and soon reached the great canal that links Holland's largest city to the sea.

There was not much traffic at such an early hour and they made it through the locks and past floodli factories to Wijk just as a good north-west swell was rolling in to the pier where they tied up their boat and jumped into the waves.

After a week at the interesting hotel Anton rented a houseboat that was tied up at a canal only a couple of hundred yards from where he would be studying.

He soon picked up the Dutch habits – especially of working hard and playing hard - and he got very good marks in his first year. He also got an abundance o waves and made some wonderful friends. And he took up a sport that he could never do in South Africa - ice skating.

In the winter of his second year the canals froze over in Friesland in the north of Holland and they were able to hold the Elfstedentocht, the skating race along the canals through eleven towns. It was over a long week-end and Anton, along with thousands of other skaters, made the journey north. He finished the course tired and exhilarated. As he raced over the finishing line he joined hands with Annaliese, a native of Friesland where they breed them tall, blonde and beautiful.

The next week-end she came down to Amsterdam to see him and, with confidence and style, he showed her round "his" town. They had their first kiss on a footbridge over a dreamy, tree lined canal not a hundred and fifty yards from his university.

As their lips touched in the moonlight Anton reflected on his good fortune in being a surfer-skater-student in the fair city of Amsterdam. The next day, when he made his weekly phone call to his parents, his father asked him how things were going and had he yet appreciated that he had won the first prize in life?

"More than that," he replied. "The first prize *cum laude*

THE POINT OF MANY NAMES

It had always been known simply as "The Point". The hillside came down to the rocks which protruded into the Pacific for a few yards before disappearing rather suddenly under the water. From the rocky point a wave formed at low tide which, although the best in the bay, would have been even better and would have held up for longer if the point had not fallen away so deeply.

The Point was an hour and a half's drive from Auckland, the largest city in New Zealand, and therein lay the reason why it was starting to become popular. It was situated at the end of the seaside town of Colonsay which, ever since the first settlers arrived there from the Scottish Highlands in 1860, had been a sleepy hollow where the locals maintained a tightly knit rural community in their little piece of paradise.

Then the worst thing happened; at the urging of the local shopkeepers the authorities sealed the dirt road over the hill that linked Colonsay with the outside world. This brought it within the dangerous band of being one and a half hours from a major city and changed the character of the place forever. Urban folk always insist on having their week-end holiday houses within an hour and a half of their city but no further and Colonsay, with its nice new road, was now within that circumference of convenience. Now that these city slickers could drive there easily on a Friday night and return on Sunday evening the number of houses in Colonsay began to mushroom and development was stimulated which, of course, was the whole point of building the road.

With development came sleaze and corruption as councillors began to take backhanders from land developers to give the right zoning decisions and building permits. And the small local surfing crew, who had names like Mad Mac, Dingbat and Quick Nick, began to feel like strangers in their own town.

The worst thing to happen was when the council planning committee, in return for the usual bribes, gave its approval for a four storey block of "luxury" apartments to be built not only above The Point but right on it. That put an end to all the little *après-surf* parties on the small stretch of sand above the rocks where the boys liked to roll a spliff and the girls sunbathed topless and sometimes bottomless.

The millionaire developer who built the structure let it be known that he now owned The Point and surfers were no longer welcome. He built a barbed wire fence around the building site which intruded on to the rocks and then, being a skinflint, took away all the beach sand and used it to make concrete. The hillside above the point was denuded of all vegetation while pneumatic drills, the noise of explosions and clouds of dust became the order of the day.

Dingbat and his friends could no longer sit at the top of the rocks although they still rode the waves off The Point from where they could watch the ugly monstrosity take shape.

The developer put the word around that this block of four "exclusive" apartments, known as "Bellevue", was so soundly built and luxurious that only the rich need apply to view the plans. This, of course, appealed to some philistines with more money than taste and it was not long before a mysterious American millionaire put down a deposit for the ground floor apartment while the developer announced in the local newspaper that he and his family were going to live on the first floor "which leaves only two more in this most exclusive of developments".

Some weeks later a middle-aged opera singer called Delilah Revelly bought the top flat. On the scales she weighed a little over twenty-four stone – and that was without her clothes on! She informed the developer that she would be bringing in a grand piano "so that I can play and sing by the seaside". His reaction was to say that the building would have to be strengthened to support the grand piano when, in fact, the real reason for the reinforcement was to support the bulk that was Delilah Revelly.

The last of the apartments was taken by a senior detective-sergeant who had made his money in the Drug Squad, reselling on the black market most of the drugs that he and his equally crooked colleagues confiscated from dealers while taking regular bribes from other dealers in return for not busting them. Like most drug cops he was a coarse and arrogant bully whose presence in the town was widely resented – especially by the surfing community who did not relish the prospect of surfing The Point under the beady eye of someone whom they simply called "The Pig".

However, it wasn't long before it became all but impossible to surf there anyway because the American millionaire turned out to be a golfing freak who had a truckload of golf balls delivered every Friday afternoon. He would then use them to practise his swing. The only problem was that every ball was used only once as it was

94

put on a tee on his balcony and then whacked into the sea.

Poor old Dingbat was hit on the head but, when he went to complain, he was told by the Texan that, if he didn't like being hit on the head by golf balls, then he should wear a motor-bike helmet in the water or else go and surf somewhere else.

The developer chimed in from the upstairs balcony that he now owned The Point and the surfers should not come trespassing on the waves. Dingbat replied with a four lettered word which brought The Pig on to his balcony with a threat to arrest Dingbat for offensive language. The cop then came down on to the rocks and shook Dingbat by the shoulders, whispering in his ear that, if either he or any of his friends ever spoiled the view again by surfing off The Point, he would plant enough hard drugs on all of them to have them locked away for years. "I am well-known and respected by the judges for the quality of the evidence I have given over many years as a senior police officer and they always believe the police – especially in drug cases," said The Pig as he reflected on all those who had crossed him over the years and had finished up behind bars as a result of what he had planted on them and the perjured evidence that he had then given in court.

And so surfing at The Point was reduced to those days when the golfer was visiting America and The Pig was away doing God knows what.

The one who gave them the least trouble was Delilah who sang so loudly that she could be heard by fishing boats a mile away. On hot days she would stand on her balcony in a one-piece swimsuit that had been custom made for her by a tent manufacturer in Auckland.

"She should be in the circus," declared Nick, "dancing with Tom Thumb. You never know what you're going to see when you come surfing at Crazy Point." This was the new name that they had given to their favourite surfing spot.

However, surfers are a hardy and persistent breed and, despite the difficulties, they still surfed Crazy Point when the golfer and The Pig were away. And when the surf was really good they would even risk missiles and abuse to ride its nicely formed waves.

It was during one such session on a Saturday afternoon that they at last got their own back. The golfer's apartment was closed up as he was in America and the developer was away ruining another beach resort further up the coast.

The Pig was entertaining some of his drug squad colleagues on the second floor balcony and occasionally they would throw down a full beer can in order to hit a surfer. Delilah was singing the lead song from *Carmen* with her parrot on her shoulder. Dingbat was surfing with Nick and Mac while their girl-friends were on the town beach about a quarter of a mile away as that was as close as they could now get to Crazy Point.

There was a lull in the waves and Dingbat and his friends were discussing how many of their slim hipped girl-friends would amount to the same weight on the scales as Delilah.

Although the waves had been rolling in all morning the sea was now as flat as a pancake. And ever so calm. In fact, none of them had ever seen the temperamental ocean so eerily placid. Suddenly dogs started barking. Delilah's poodle began the orchestra and, like a chain of bonfires, the cry was taken up all along the road and into town as pooches barked for all they were worth.

Then it happened. A rumbling sound that permeated land, sea and sky and got louder and louder. From their vantage point about fifty yards out in the blue Pacific they could see the town and the hills shaking like a jelly. Boom! It sounded as if all the guns at Alamein had gone off at the same time as the hills shook and banged against each other.

It drowned out Delilah's singing and Dingbat looked up to see if she had come out on to the balcony. He also wondered if she had fallen off the piano stool which, of course, would have explained the earthquake. As his eyes turned towards the top floor of Bellevue the movie really came to life as he saw with his own eyes the tower like structure fall in upon itself and then come crashing down on to the rocks and into the sea. He thought he could see the red of Delilah's dress through the dust cloud of crashing masonry. Of all those who were in the Bellevue when the earthquake struck only the parrot survived. Poor Delilah and The Pig and his fellow drug cops all went to a watery grave.

Then Act Two began. Nick was the first to see the wall of water about ten feet high that was speeding in from out at sea. First the quake and then the tidal wave.

Above the roar he screamed to his friends to paddle towards the town beach which, being sandy, would be a better place to land than the rocks. And anyway he didn't relish the prospect of sharing an ocean grave off Crazy Point with The Pig.

In the incredibly short time they had before meeting the tidal wave they paddled for all they were worth so that, when it struck, they were about two hundred yards off the beach and ready to "go with the flow".

As the moving mountain of water was about to smother them each took a deep breath and managed to emerge safely both higher and shoreward from where they started. The force of the rushing water drove them towards town. Soon they found themselves being swept up the main street with Dingbat and Nick finishing up clinging to the upstairs verandah posts of the two storey wooden hotel, which was still shaking vigorously, and Mac landing on the roof of the chemist shop and hugging its chimney.

As they clung to their posts they watched the water drown the town before emptying into the lagoon on the other side. Then, as fast as the water came, it went out again, exposing rocks and reefs that no one had ever seen before.

As the aftershocks seemed to be diminishing in both noise and intensity Dingbat made his way across the floor of the bar. The smell of liquor was strong as most of the bottles had been smashed; all he managed to find was a sturdy bottle of Napoleon brandy from which he took a couple of much needed swigs to calm his nerves. He then returned to the verandah and offered it to Nick.

The ground and buildings continued to shake as Nick and Dingbat tied their boards to the verandah post by the legrope and then went looking for Mac. By using their secret coded hooting sound – two longs and a short, followed by a long and a short - they soon found their

98

friend and coaxed him down from the sloping roof via a drainpipe. The ground was slimy from the visit of the tidal wave and was starting to smell of raw sewerage.

People with broken bones and other injuries were screaming out and the three surfers began removing bodies from the rubble, tying bandages and comforting the dying. Then, above the noise of rumble, explosions and screams, they heard a distant siren from over the other side of the hill. Then some more and it was not long before a major rescue operation was under way.

The seriously wounded were taken to the Auckland Hospital by helicopter and ambulance while others were treated in a field hospital that was set up in the camping ground.

As soon as the emergency services took over Nick, Mac, and Dingbat made their way round to Crazy Point in order to satisfy their curiosity. After all, no part of the countryside meant more to them than their historic surfing spot – despite all the ups and downs

As they wound their way around Point Road they looked out at sea and saw that Mother Ocean had resumed her usual state – a little choppy and waves breaking off the point again. But the waves were much bigger than normal. They were also cleaner and seemed to be holding up for longer.

It was then that they realised that, out of all the death and destruction, Huey had sent them a special gift; all the concrete and masonry that had gone into the building of expensive Bellevue had deposited itself in the relatively deep water off the rocky point to form the most perfectly formed reef that any of them had ever seen.

They found the corpse of the red clad Delilah floating a few yards out, the parrot hovering over her and making a great commotion. But there was no sign of the cops; they had been buried beneath the masonry and would at last be of some use to mankind by forming part of the foundations of the new reef.

They dived into the sea to bring Delilah to the shore; it was like towing an aircraft carrier but they eventually made it and, with the help of a winch and some thick rope, managed to pull her up on to the rocks. Then Nick went diving along the new reef to see if there was any sign of the cops; there wasn't but he did see one ingredient of the reef that by some miracle had not been smashed – the grand piano. It was so positioned that its length ran along the top of the reef in a straight line. Huey could not have arranged it better.

When he got back to the rocks he saw that the cleanest part of the wave was where it broke over the piano. It was then that Dingbat spoke. He said that Crazy Point was now their's again and in a much better state than before.

"Let's not call it Crazy Point any more," said Nick. "It's now a new point and so deserves to have a new name."

"Like what?"

"Piano Point. And I'm going to be the first one to ride it".

THE PERILS OF SUCCESS

August in Britain is known as "the silly season" because most people are away on holiday and there is nothing to put in the newspapers except silly stories like sightings of the Loch Ness monster and the woman who gave birth to her fourth set of quads.

At the offices of the Filth newspaper, just off Fleet Street, the editor, Eddie Stick, was telling Felicity Fickle that there was a surf contest taking place down at Ocean Beach in Cornwall and would she like to go down and report on it because for the first time a British surfer was expected to win.

Twenty-five year old Felicity was an ambitious and conscientious reporter who would do virtually anything to get ahead in her journalistic career. She was good-looking without being ravenously beautiful but her face sometimes assumed an air of hardness. Her problem was that she was too "career oriented" and this had robbed her of much of her femininity. But she did have a vivacious personality.

After drawing her expenses she caught the train down, presented herself at the Press box, received her accreditation and then sat on the stand to view the action.

As a city girl Felicity had never seen anyone surf before except in films. Nor had she been to the beach more than half a dozen times in her life. So, at least she would be approaching it from a fresh and objective viewpoint.

Thrilled at having a reporter come all the way from London, the contest organisers and even some of the pro surfers went out of their way to be friendly to her. On the first night she was taken to dinner by the sponsor's publicity officer and had some of the finer points of surfing explained to her.

The next day she roamed around the stands and along the beach as she watched the action both in and out of the water. Everybody seemed friendly and natural which was quite a change from the superficial world that she knew in London.

Her reporter's eye could see that there was great style and beauty in surfing and she quickly came to the conclusion that some of the well-built hunks in their boardshorts were the handsomest men she had ever seen. Especially the one with blond, curly hair one who, as part of a small bet as well as a lark, took off his boardshorts and rode a couple of waves in the natural state – much to the delight of the crowd, especially the female section of it.

She later found out that it was Byron Sheen, the one who was expected to win the contest and the reason why she had come all the way down to Cornwall.

That night she was invited to a party where everyone was nice to her, offering her food, drink, smokes and conversation.

On Finals Day she watched from the Press Box as Byron thrilled the crowd with a display of tube riding and aerials that seemed as reckless as they were professional. No one could match this performance – not even the pro from Hawaii who surfed his whole heat with a bright red hibiscus behind his right ear. Felicity found herself cheering with all the others when Byron was announced the contest winner.

The end-of-contest party was held in the Grand Pavilion that opened on to the wide beach. It was crowded with sweating, suntanned surfers and their spunky girl-friends, all trying to squeeze as much pleasure as they could out of these last few hours of contest week.

Ever the reporter, Felicity did the rounds to absorb something of the atmosphere. In a dark corner she saw a couple of guys laying out a line on a coffee table and rolling up a banknote.

On the dance floor she moved to the techno beat. One of the partygoers, who was a little the worse for drink, came stumbling past her and tripped over. The surfer, whose leg he tripped over, put on an expression of mock anger and raised his fist. They were both laughing and then the guy with his fist raised fell down on his friend and they had a fun wrestling match for a few minutes before getting up.

Then someone offered Felicity a pill and she took it. Things started to improve rapidly. For one thing, she spotted Byron Sheen a few feet away and made her way over to kiss him on the cheek. And then on the lips. He too was in a mellow mood and responded warmly. This was nothing more than she expected for, as an up and coming reporter on the Filth, she usually got her own way. She believed that a woman could now have everything – a high paying job, independence, whatever man she wanted and an infinitely stimulating social life. And Byron was part of her scheme – at least for to-night.

He knew that she was from the Filth but the warmth of her body and the intimacy of her wandering hands tended to dull his judgement. And anyway, he couldn't get rid of her.

By 1 a.m. the champion was starting to feel tired; after all, he had surfed two heats that day as well as the "expression session", taken a shower of champagne, made the victor's speech and danced through the night. He had had his eye on another girl earlier on but, with Felicity all over him like a rash, it just seemed easier to stay on this road instead of taking a fresh turn which might not lead to the same place.

When the music finally stopped he declared that it was time to return to his hotel which was only a few yards along the beach. Felicity made up some cock and bull story of how her hotel was so far away that she would never find it at this hour of night and there were no taxis and she was frightened of being mugged on the way home and all the rest of it. Byron really had no choice but to suggest that she spend the night in his room. Suffice to say they slept together and made tender love.

On the train back to London Felicity set up her laptop on the table in front of her seat so that she could write her report for the editor to fill a page or two. She was still feeling happy from all the good vibes she had got from the surfers and, as the train sped through the picturesque countryside of Cornwall and Devon, her mellow mood continued as she looked out the window at the green fields and grey, stone cottages.

The next morning she handed her report to the Editor. This is what he read: "The surf contest at Ocean Beach was won by the up and coming British surfer, Byron Sheen. In front of his home crowd this stylish waverider conquered all before him and stood on the winner's platform beneath a shower of champagne that was sprayed on him by his fellow surfers. If horse racing is the sport of kings, then surely surfing must be the sport of princes.

Byron Sheen is just as stylish out of the water as in it. In his favourite element he loves tearing up the ocean to thrill the spectators on the beach.

Although surfing is a professional sport it is not in the big money league and the atmosphere down at Ocean Beach was homely and informal and without the massive security and impersonal organisation that are now the norm at football matches and international golf and tennis tournaments. Everybody seemed to know everybody else and the surfers were having as much fun at the after-surf parties as in the waves. The large number of kids who were present on the beach augurs well for this growing and ever more popular sport.

Contestants from Brazil, France, Australia, the United States and Portugal gave colour and an international flavour to the contest, never more so than the Hawaiian who surfed with a flower behind his ear.

Although the judging in surfing is somewhat subjective there can be no argument but that the best surfer won the contest. Byron Sheen has been on the international circuit for two years and has surfed in contests in France, Mauritius, South Africa, Australia and Hawaii. This was only his second major contest win but, if this week's performance is anything to go by, the sporting world will be hearing a lot more of this young man in the years to come.

Byron was brought up at Ocean Beach although he went to school at Hatfield in Devon; this, it should be noted, is the same public school that educated England's current fast bowler, Ted Grimshaw.

The organisers say that this is the most successful contest that Ocean Beach has ever hosted and next year they intend to have two contests back-to-back – in other words, a fortnight's festival of surfing."

There were another two pages but the Editor didn't bother reading them. He looked up with a disinterested air, screwed the pages into a ball and threw them into his wastepaper basket.

"I paid your expenses to spend three days down in Cornwall and this is all you can come up with. Not one of our ten million readers would bother reading past the first paragraph of this sugary crap. I want a demolition job on this little bastard. Our readers are mean, nasty, jealous, sexually frustrated people; that's why we have to have the Page Three girl every day. They all live in grotty, two roomed council flats and they absolutely hate anyone who has anything more than they've got. Our job is to feed their envy and prejudices by destroying their betters one by one. Find his weak points; then we can build him up for a couple of paragraphs and then crush him with some choice adjectives, innuendo and anything else negative we can think of. I want this ex-public school sporting champion to be Public Enemy Number One. With his fortunate background, surfing ability and obvious good looks he is tailor made for public odium. There are no longer any public hangings and the Filth is the last refuge of those who enjoy the destruction of others.

Stick to our time-tested formula which is never to write anything nice about anyone except nurses, policemen, firefighters and ambulance drivers. They're the only heroes we can present to our lower class readership. Everyone else is dog's meat. How many times do I have to tell you young reporters that nurses, policemen, firefighters and ambulance drivers are on one side of the fence and everyone else is on the other. Even doctors; they're too rich and too well-qualified for the liking of most people and so they have to be vilified too. Every readers' poll tells us that the only ones they ever want to hear good things about are nurses, policemen, firefighters and ambulance drivers."

Knowing that her job was on the line, Felicity returned to her desk and started typing again. An hour later she handed the Editor her second version. It was headlined "Time to Ban Surfing".

"This week I had one of the most eye-popping experiences of my life. I was sent down to Ocean Beach in Cornwall to report on what was billed as a "surf contest" but which, in fact, was an orgy of drunkenness, drug taking, immorality and violence. One wonders why they bothered putting heats in the water when it was quite obvious that the only reason anybody was there was to take part in the non-stop debauchery through the night.

The British public in general and Filth readers in particular need to be told that their children are in grave moral danger by going into the waves and mixing with the types who ride surfboards. People like Byron Sheen, who won the contest by surfing naked. Yes, stark naked! Not even a figleaf! But what is even more alarming is that the police did not even arrest him for obscene exposure.

We at the Filth say that, instead of swanning off to some sex tourist place for the next contest, this flagrant lawbreaker should be put behind bars and taught a lesson. What sort of example was he setting to all the young children on the beach whose innocent eyes were exposed to the vile horror of being forced to look at his private parts? Is it any wonder that so many young kids were crying and screaming and grandmothers were fainting and falling down on the sand?

Surfing is for toffs and the only reason why Byron Sheen can afford to travel the world circuit is because he comes from a moneyed family. He went to Hatfield! This sport for the rich is an affront to the new egalitarian mood that is sweeping through Britain and destroying privilege in its path. Like hunting, surfing should be banned. Why should a privileged class be able to go out on their expensive surfboards while wage earners – people like nurses, policemen, firefighters and ambulance drivers – have to stay on land and perform their difficult and dangerous tasks of keeping our society safe for so little reward?

Among the sights that I saw at Ocean Beach was a surfer from Hawaii who wore a flower behind his ear. If he is that unsure of his sexual identity, one wonders why he didn't enter the women's section of the contest. He is typical of the transsexuals who flaunt their all but naked bodies in the surf.

At the contest party on Sunday night there were mafiosi drug dealers cruising the dance floor and forcing children as young as twelve to buy hard drugs. The lines of cocaine stretched across every table while there were more pills than one would find in Guy's Hospital.

And the violence! Two drunken louts had a vicious fight on the dance floor less than a foot from where I was standing. Blood spurted out from the knife wounds and spattered on the clothes of others who were mostly too "out of it" to know what was happening.

Surfing is ceasing to be a sport and is fast becoming a social problem. It was introduced to Britain in the 1960s by Australian lifesavers who came over to patrol our beaches in summer. Unfortunately, these descendants of convicts brought with them their great, long planks of fibreglass, thereby exposing the youth of Britain to this new form of colonial decadence.

The fact is that Britain got along very well for centuries without this dangerous and socially destructive activity so why do we suddenly need it now? The sooner the government plucks up enough courage to ban surfing, the better it will be for the moral welfare of the nation."

"Ah, yes", said the Editor as he finished reading it. "This is better. And I like the bit about how disgusting it was to have this flea bitten exhibitionist show off his private parts. Of course, I won't be able to run it on Page Three as we might be accused of hypocrisy and its not juicy enough for Page One. But Page Seven should do. By then our semi-literate readers will have forgotten what they saw on Page Three as research has shown that their attention span doesn't extend more than a couple of pages at a time."

Pleased that his reporter had at last justified the train fare down to Cornwall, Eddie Stick looked at his watch and saw that it was nearly lunch time. He suggested to Felicity that they go out for a bite to eat at the bar on the corner which had dim lights and young hostesses wearing gym slips and nothing else. The ever ambitious Felicity was delighted to be asked to lunch by her esteemed editor.

While Felicity had been typing the second piece Mr. Stick had retrieved the first effort from the wastepaper basket and re-read it. "Why would she be drooling over this young punk called Byron Sheen?" he wondered.

This doyen of the tabloid press felt that she was holding something back and he was determined to find out what it was. Or, to put it more accurately, to find out if it contained any material for a Page One.

Through the sweet smell of cigar smoke they were shown to a table in an alcove where they ordered a couple of bottles of Bordeaux. Carried away by the occasion of "lunching with the Editor", Felicity drank every glass of wine that Stick poured for her – a total of six. Just enough to loosen her tongue.

After finishing their steak sandwiches the lecherous Stick let his foot touch her's as he stared straight into her eyes. "When was the last time you had sex?" was the question he fired at her.

The suddenness and intimacy of the question threw her off balance and, with her editor's feet rubbing against her's coupled with the alcohol, she could hardly avoid making a straightforward answer. "Sunday night." She replied.

"With Byron Sheen, wasn't it?"

"Yes."

"But it was not consensual sex?"

"What do you mean?"

"He raped you, didn't he?"

"Oh, I wouldn't say that."

Stick pulled out a cheque book and put it on the table. "What sort of car do you drive?" he asked.

"A Ford Escort."

"Would you like a Ferrari?"

"What do you mean?"

He tore out a cheque, filled it in for "fifty thousand pounds" and signed it. It was more than Felicity earned in a year.

"This is your's right now," said Stick, "provided you swear an affidavit to our in-house lawyer upstairs that Byron Sheen raped you. Hell, there were only two of you in the room and it's just his word against your's. And nobody is going to believe him as it was only the day before that he had taken off his kit in the water to signify his intentions."

Felicity did not reply immediately as she was thinking. She didn't want to behave like a prostitute – like so many of the other young women on the reporting staff who, because of the irregular hours of journalism, were able to supplement their earnings by walking the streets of King's Cross at unusual hours. And, of course, if ever they got a well-known client, Stick would pay them £50,000 for a Page One story. All part of the wonderful new world of "chequebook journalism".

Then she thought of the Ferrari. She had always wanted a red one and now was her chance. A chance that might never come again. "But I wouldn't want my name to appear in the paper," she said.

"It won't. Under section 4 (1) of the Sexual Offences (Amendment) Act 1976 any woman who makes an allegation of rape is protected by law from ever being named."

"Even if the allegation is proved to be false?"

"Yes. That's the beauty of it. The man's name is plastered across the front pages of the press as soon as the allegation – true or false – is made but the woman can never be named. As editor of the Filth I have often used this law to get women who need a bit of money to make a false allegation against a celebrity to give us our Page One for the day. You're very lucky that, because he won the contest, your little Byron is – for this week at least – sufficiently newsworthy to be named in a rape case on Page One. If he hadn't won and if it wasn't the silly season with so little news, I would not be making you the offer."

"Won't it be too late? I thought one was required to report rape immediately after it happened."

"Nonsense. The law allows weeks, months – even years - to pass before the victim can bring herself to mention it. What we'll do is publish your second piece – the demolition job – in to-morrow's edition so that our readers can be introduced to him and learn to hate him. The next day we'll follow it up with a Page One rape. Perfect. A tabloid editor's dream."

"So what do I do after swearing the affidavit?"

"Find the Ferrari of your choice. If the matter goes to trial, you merely repeat in the witness box what you have stated in the affidavit - namely, that at no time did you consent to sexual intercourse."

Felicity thought about it for a moment. Cornwall now seemed a long way away and she would probably never see him again anyway. For the sake of protecting someone in a one night stand should she turn down a Ferrari?

"Very well," she replied, "let's go up and I'll swear the affidavit".

"Before the ink is dry you will have the cheque."

Two days later the surfing world of Britain was rocked by the allegations against their new champion that were plastered across Page One of the Filth and

112

continued on Pages 4, 5, 6, 7 and 8. It was the usual "Sports Champion in Rape Allegation" that had "graced" the front page of the Filth on so many previous occasions.

Poor Byron was later found guilty, his earlier lark of surfing naked having persuaded the jurors that he was some sort of mad sex fiend, and he was sentenced to seven years' imprisonment with a firm warning from the judge to surfers not to "take advantage of vulnerable young women like the complainant. I am glad that, in this case at least, justice has indeed been done." And every one of the Filth's ten million readers agreed. It was the price that Byron paid for succeeding as a surfing champion instead of being one of the nurses, policemen, firefighters or ambulance drivers.

JUSTICE WITHOUT BLOOD

Porpoise Point was surfers' territory. It was reached by an unformed road where hardly anyone else ever ventured and in the big clearing at the end the guys could park their cars, vans and beach buggies under the shade of the gum and pine trees while they went out into the waves. At least that had been the situation for forty years. However, the local council had recently installed parking meters all along the sealed road that led to the dirt track of Porpoise Point. They then put up "No Parking" signs all along the dirt road and in the clearing at the end so as to force everyone to use the meters.

On the day that the signs went up none of the surfers took any notice of them as, having always parked there without bothering anybody, they intended to continue to do so. The next day the crew were all out in the big six foot plus surf that was breaking over the submerged reef off the point. The waves were clean and glassy and the smiles on the faces of those who scored some good rides said it all.

When the wind turned onshore about midday they started to paddle in to the small beach as it was time for lunch, work or a snooze in the sun.

Upon reaching their vehicles they found that every one of them had been given a parking ticket with the standard fine which, for young chaps just out of school, was quite considerable.

They could even see the little rat in the uniform as he was writing the last ticket. And they knew him! He had been at the local high school where, because of his acne and his generally pathetic nature, he had been picked on more than anyone else. And now he was

114

getting his own back. His name was Willy but at school they all called him Dilly as it seemed more appropriate for such a moron.

Matt and some of the others went up and asked him what the hell he thought he was doing as they had parked their cars there to surf the point for years and so had their fathers before them without being the slightest nuisance to man or beast.

A smug look came over Dilly's face as he stood to his full height (all five foot, three of him!) in his uniform with all its shiny buttons and badges. "You've broken the law by parking in a 'No Parking' area and my job is to enforce it."

Simon had to restrain Matt from lashing out with his fists but the verbal barrage they launched was pretty impressive and should really have gone into the Guinness Book of Records for the greatest volley of four lettered words ever fired over the course of five minutes.

"We're not paying," spat Damien as he screwed up his ticket.

"Then the matter will go to court and you'll feel the full force of the law. If all else fails, you'll be in prison." Dilly had a positive leer on his pockmarked face as he uttered these words. Then, having completed his mission, he made off down the dirt road, dodging a few flying stones as he went.

After the rest of them had come out of the waves they had an informal meeting around their ticketed cars. Everybody was furious at being punished for doing something that had been perfectly legal for decades and the fact that the particular agent of the mischief was a jumped up little so-in-so like Dilly only made it worse.

One of the victims was Jez who was a builder by trade. He opened the doors of his ticketed van, got out his ladder and hammer, and knocked down all the new signs. But that would not get them out of their fines. With tickets on more than twenty vehicles, the council had bagged a nice little chunk of surfers' money.

All their wild and angry proposals were knocked down by Alastair, the owner of the local surf shop who was older than the others and was liked and respected by them. He was a man of absolute integrity and had a very strong sense of right and wrong. And he knew that, to ticket the cars of surfers while they were out in the waves and causing no harm to anybody, was about as wrong as it can get. His apparently genial and easygoing nature concealed some pretty strong urges. Like Sir Francis Drake, he was "the mildest mannered man who ever slit a throat".

Alastair advised everyone to contain their anger while he would go to the council and explain the situation, saying that, since the signs had only just gone up, there should have been a period of grace before the tickets were issued.

The council scoffed at his suggestion that the tickets be scrapped. "Why should surfers receive preferential treatment? You're damned lucky that we allow you to surf in the waves at all. They are also the council's property and, if you don't stop whinging, we'll impose a tax on all who use them," declared Councillor Block.

"But we weren't hurting anyone or blocking any traffic. If we're forced to use the meters, we'll have to walk a quarter of a mile to get to the waves."

"Do you good. Might teach you to respect the law."

Having failed in his first effort Alastair told the surfers that they had no choice but to pay up "but only once".

"Why only once? That little piece of filth will come back every day. He sees it as pay-back time for all the times he was picked on at school."

"Listen," said Alastair, "pay up and for the next couple of days we'll park our vehicles on the meters. Then on Thursday I want everyone to park here in the clearing so as to lure him back. He won't be able to resist the chance to ticket us all a second time."

"And then?"

"Wait and see."

Alastair had lived on this part of the coast for a long time and knew all sorts of people for miles around. One day earlier in the year he had been driving north when he witnessed an accident between a police car and a motor cyclist. The cop car took the bend too fast and collided with the bike that was travelling in its correct lane and almost certainly within the speed limit.

The cop who was driving the police car was killed but his passenger and the motor cyclist both survived their injuries. Of course, the police lied and lied and lied in order to get their manslaughter charge against the motor cyclist to stick and it was only Alastair's truthful evidence that persuaded the jury to acquit.

After the case the bike rider, a member of a motor cycle gang called the Deadly Dreadnoughts, took Alastair for a drink at the pub next door to the court. One of the things he told Alastair was, "If ever you're in a spot of bother, just remember that me and the

Dreadnoughts owe you one. You only have to ask. We always enjoy a bit of action."

Alastair had put it in the back of his mind but now decided that it was time to take up the offer. It was, he realised, the only way to protect the surfers' traditional right to park at their surf spot. And, if there was going to be any "action", it was better to get out-of-towners to do it so as not to cast any suspicion on the local surfing crew.

The next day he drove up to the Dreadnoughts' headquarters where he was welcomed like a long lost brother. He explained the predicament and noted the glimmer of excitement in their eyes at the prospect of action in a good cause.

"Just one condition," he stipulated. "No blood. Okay?"

"Yes, brother, no blood. But we can still promise that he won't harass you again. And nor will any of the other parking wardens; they'll be too bloody scared."

"I've told the boys Thursday."

"Right. Just make sure they're all out in the waves for a couple of hours so as not to incriminate themselves."

Thursday dawned bright and clear and the deep blue ocean seemed to shimmer in the sun. Even though the waves were not as big as usual everyone stayed in the water for a long time. The clearing where all the cars were parked was deserted – or so it seemed.

Although there had not been any vehicles in the clearing for a couple of days Dilly still came by, checking first to see if any of the parking meters had expired and then walking up the dirt road to see if there were any surfers' vehicles although by now he sincerely believed that he had frightened them all away. Ah, the power of a uniform!

Imagine his surprise – and delight - when he saw not twenty but more than thirty vehicles nestling under the trees. Since he was paid on commission he had the double good fortune of being able to earn a record amount and having the satisfaction of annoying even more surfers. And, since they were all out surfing, he would be able to do his ticketing and then get away before all the abusive, violent drivers returned to their cars. What he didn't know was that there were Dreadnoughts lurking among the trees.

They waited until he had ticketed two cars and a van. By then he was as close to the forest as he was likely to get. While he had his head down writing the fourth ticket three of the masked and rubber gloved Dreadnoughts emerged ever so quietly from the trees and knocked him to the ground with a bit of the old martial arts. One of them put a tennis ball in his mouth to stop him crying out. No blood. Just as Alastair had stipulated.   They then dragged him deeper into the trees to avoid any risk of being spotted by a passer-by.

Next they stripped him of his fancy uniform; in fact, they stripped him naked. Then a fourth Dreadnought arrived from the other end of the woods, carrying – of all things – an aluminium window frame with the glass still inside it and a small bag.

Dilly was afraid that they would smash the glass over his head but that would have breached the "No blood" rule. Instead, these mad Dreadnoughts took from the bag several tubes of Super glue and started squirting it on the large window frame.

They then picked up the naked man and pressed him against the sticky pane – shoulders, buttocks and the backs of his legs. A few seconds later he was bonded to the glass in a very big way, the hairs on the backs of his legs providing extra adhesion.

They removed the tennis ball from his mouth but took the added precaution of dabbing a bit of Super glue on his lips before pressing them together. They then carried the window pane and its "Siamese twin" to the clearing where they laid it down on the ground next to the last car that had been ticketed so that Dilly could sunbathe – sunny side up. Dilly was not actually in any pain although he couldn't move, couldn't talk and – worst of all (for him) – couldn't write any more tickets.

Mission accomplished, they dashed back through the woods to where their van was parked in a secluded spot.

It was more than half an hour before Dilly was found on his bed of hot glass by a couple of fishermen who were returning from the rocks with their rods and their catch.

At first they laughed as they thought they had come across some mad, naked exhibitionist who had some weird need to show off his private parts on a public road. "Perhaps he thinks he's a piece of living art," said Bill.

"Not with acne like that," replied his mate.

"Are you okay, small cock?" they said as they walked past.

No answer. Just a groan without the lips parting. Upon further investigation they found that the naked man and the large window pane were one and the same part. Bill walked over to his van, which had been ticketed, and called the police and ambulance on his mobile phone, saying that, although he didn't know the circumstances, "there's a right one out here who is stuck to a piece of glass".

"You mean a piece of glass is stuck to him? What part of his body?"

"Most of it."

By now the Dreadnoughts were fifty miles up the road. No blood. Well, not until Dilly got to the hospital and the surgeons found that there were really only two ways of separating him from the pane. They could either cut away all the skin on his back, buttocks and the backs of his legs or they could smash the glass into pieces and then pluck them out bit by bit, taking much of the skin with them.

After several days of lengthy and difficult surgery and endless skin grafts Dilly came out of hospital but he had to resign his job of patrolling the streets and ticketing cars because he could not walk for several months. The other parking meter wardens threatened to go on strike if they were ever asked to go up that dangerous dirt road again and the council, which was only interested in revenue, decided that it was easier to target motorists in other – and safer - parts of the town. Thus the surfers were once again free to park their cars and vans at their favourite surfing spot. As the sun went down they sat around their cars talking about it. Alastair seemed to sum up everyone's feelings when he quoted Winston Churchill's words, "Freedom sometimes has to be fought for."

UNCROWDED BALI

The same day that Jason received the timetable for his end of year exams in 2002 he went down to the travel agent and booked a two month trip to Bali, flying out only two days after his last exam. He had been saving up for it for more than two years.

Over the years Jason had heard lots of stories about Bali from others of the beach crew who had been there – its wonderful waves, the gentle, smiling Balinese people and the wild party scene at night. He had also read several books – both surfing and others – about the island and, the more he read, the more he wanted to go there.

Jason lived in Perth but his house was several miles inland from the coast. From an early age he had caught the bus down to the beach at Scarborough and learned to surf in its warm waves. Surfing was both his passion and his means of keeping fit. That was why he had been a bit of a misfit at his inland high school; being a well-tanned, slimly built surfer he was not one of the football jocks and had suffered accordingly.

In his last year at high school he had worked part-time as a petrol station attendant while in the long summer holiday between school and university he had a job working in a surf shop just across the road from the beach at Scarborough. Now he was in the first year of a B.A. course at the University of Western Australia where he was majoring in geography – a subject that had always fascinated him.

Jason was a very self-contained young man who had never been out of Australia and that was why he was so looking forward to the BIG surfing trip to Bali. By booking his flight in September to fly out in November he had got it dirt cheap – which meant that he would have more money to spend during his two months on the island. It also meant that he couldn't change it or get a refund if, for some reason, he was unable to travel.

Having purchased it, he put it away and got down to some serious study for the exams which were now less than two months away. He would work hard at university and then play hard in Bali.

However, upon waking up on the morning of Sunday, 13th October, and turning on the radio to listen to the morning's news, he was shocked to hear that a gang of Muslim terrorists had bombed the Sari Club bar in Bali and that Australian surfers – many of them from Perth – were still being pulled out of the carnage. This was not the Bali that he had been looking forward to. In one terrible, short moment his whole world seemed to have changed forever.

When Jason went downstairs for breakfast his mother asked if he still wanted to go to what she said was now a "war zone" or would he cancel his ticket?

"If I cancel, I don't get a refund," he explained.

"Listen, son, this is serious," said his father. "If you cancel, I'll compensate you for however much you spent on the ticket and you can go to some other place – like everyone else will be doing." But for two years Jason had set his heart on a Bali surfing holiday and he was not prepared to scupper it in the heat of the moment.

"I've still got another month to decide," he said. "I don't want to make a decision now that I might regret later."

That afternoon he went down to Scarborough for a surf with his mates and acquainted them with his dilemma. Some of the more easily impressionable said that he would be mad to go as he would probably come back in a body bag but the owner of the local surf shop, a worldly wise fellow who had been to Bali many times, said that lightning never strikes the same place twice and that, with other surfers being too scared to go there, it might well be a unique opportunity to ride Bali's wonderful reefs and points without the stress of a crowded line-up.

Jason seemed to sway from one point of view to the other but what persuaded him more than anything else was when he visited his grandparents and told them of his problem. They had emigrated to Australia from London in the 1950s and they knew how hard he had been saving up for this, his first trip out of Australia, and how he had set his heart on it.

"Yes, dreadful business," said his grandfather. "I've always said that all terrorists – Muslims, I.R.A., the lot of them – should be strung up and left to hang in the breeze. Then I'd cut down their dead carcasses and let the dogs feast on them. That's all they're good for."

Jason did not disagree but it did not solve his problem of whether or not to go.

"You really want to go, don't you?" said his grandmother rather sweetly.

"I think so. I was mad keen to go before this. Now I still want to go but I don't want to put myself at risk."

"There are always risks in life," she said. "While Bill was away in the Navy during the War I stuck it out in London right through the Blitz. The bombs fell almost every night for eight months – homes being destroyed, people being killed and maimed, huge fires, sirens – I'll never forget it. The great stores of Oxford Street – Selfridges, John Lewis – all bombed by the Germans. One night the fires raged all the way from Hammersmith to Romford and they burned for days. But we got through it."

"How?" asked an amazed Jason.

"Because we had a few secret weapons."

"Meaning?"

"Our superb British sense of humour, the strength of our ancient race and its time tested institutions and, of course, we did happen to have the best leader who ever trod the earth."

"Churchill?"

"God bless his name. Of course, this is bad but it is only one bomb – not like the Blitz. There is not much point in tiptoeing through life just to arrive at a safe death. By the time you're due to go I think a lot of this would have calmed down. I suggest you get on with your studies and don't look at the television as I can't see the point of showing all these dead and battered bodies on the screen night after night. There's only so much blood and guts and orchestrated sentimentality that one can take. So, if you concentrate on your exams and keep your eyes off the television, then you should be able to make a sensible judgement at the end of the day."

And that is exactly what Jason did. "Lightning never strikes the same place twice" and "Don't tiptoe through life to a safe death" – these two sentences seemed to lodge in his brain and rear their ghostly heads whenever he thought about the issue. Result: two days after his last exam Jason, with his two surfboards and a bag of clothes, checked in at Perth airport for his flight to Bali on Garuda Indonesian Airlines. It was exactly one month after the bomb went off.

There were only six passengers on the plane and he was the only surfer. Since the cabin crew outnumbered the passengers a smiling Indonesian air hostess came and sat next to him for much of the flight. She chatted to him about Bali and asked him questions about surfing, his life in Australia and why he chose to go to Bali at this particular time. She beamed when he said that he had been looking forward to it for two years and didn't see why a single bomb should be allowed to shatter such a beautiful dream.

After the plane landed at Bali's Ngurah Rai airport the wide eyed surfer was welcomed to the island by smiling immigration and customs officers who, Jason reflected, were the complete antithesis of the sour faced emigration officer who had stamped his passport at Perth airport and told him what a fool he was to be going to such a place.

There seemed to be more police and soldiers than passengers in the terminal building as the Indonesian authorities were very effectively shutting the stable door after the horse had bolted.

Outside there seemed to be a thousand taxis vying for the custom of him and the handful of other passengers who were passing through the doors – straight from the cool air conditioning of the terminal into the sticky tropical heat.

Jason rented a thatched roof cottage at Seminyak; it was nearly three miles away from the scene of devastation at the Sari Club. He also rented a motor bike so that he could travel to distant waves with his surfboard slung over his shoulder. For both these

126

important items – accommodation and wheels – he paid a mere pittance. Bali after the bomb was a "buyer's market".

There was a beach break in front of the cottage where he surfed most afternoons and was the only one out. Surfers had deserted the island in their thousands and it seemed that, thanks to the travel warnings of Western governments, no more were coming in.

Jason used his motor bike to do some exploring. He drove up to Ubud and to Mount Agung where the gods were reputed to live although he reckoned that they must have all been asleep on the night the bomb went off.

He surfed Kuta Reef, Padang Padang, Uluwatu, Bingan and other breaks. The surf was consistently good, the water was warm and the waves were uncrowded. He met an older American surfer called Ronnie who had been coming to Bali for almost thirty years. He assured Jason that the crowd situation in the waves was now back to what it was in 1974 when he first came to the island. "Think of it, man, you're back in the best days of Bali. Its very beginnings as a surfing destination. I never thought we'd be so lucky."

"We might be lucky but others haven't been."

"Oh yes, I know it's bad form to gloat when so many are suffering but I can't help thinking that the bomb was an accident waiting to happen."

"What do you mean?"

"When I first came here this island was heaven. It was like playing in the Garden of Eden. Then came more and more tourists, greed, development, petrol fumes, night clubs full of drunken footballers, prostitution, a McDonalds, high rise hotels and countless other manifestations of our ugly Western society. The whole place was shooting ahead like a meteor on a disaster course and the bomb will at least check this onward rush of madness and give people pause for thought.

In its long history Bali has survived several such convulsions and, terrible though the bomb was, it was by no means the worst thing that has happened here. There was the *puputan* of 1906 when the Balinese killed themselves in the face of a Dutch army, then the brutal occupation of the island in the Second World War by the Japs and then the killing of more than ten thousand people on Kuta Beach during the turmoil of 1965 and now the Sari Club bomb. And out of every disaster comes new life. That is the essence of reincarnation which is the mainstay of Balinese belief. Out of death comes life."

Some of the Balinese asked Jason what he thought of the massacre and did he think that the tourists would ever come back to Bali. Having built their economy and indeed their lives around the tourist industry, they had now seen it taken away from them in one cruel blow. Although Western television showed the victims of the bomb being put on planes to be flown back to their own countries Jason could see that Bali itself was also a victim because it had lost its main source of income. And there was not much to fall back on – just a few coconuts and fish and the mangy looking cows in the fields.

He soon realised that the destruction of the economy was as much an object of the bombers as the killing of Westerners for Bali is a Hindu island and, since Moslem militants hate anyone who is not of their

128

own intolerant religion, they were just as happy to impoverish Hindus as to kill Westerners.

Jason did not go to any large bars or night clubs; most of them had closed down anyway. After long and tiring sessions in the waves his nights were spent at small native restaurants, being served rice dishes and delicious fruit salads under the coconut trees and leisurely talking, playing cards and passing the time with the handful of other doughty Westerners who defied their government's "travel warnings" against going to Bali and, as a result, were savouring the delights of one of the world's most beautiful islands where they were treated like kings and queens by the locals.

"Bali is a land of extremes", Ronnie had said to him. "*Kaja* and *kelod*. *Kaja* is the direction of the mountains where the gods live and goodness resides whereas *kelod* is the other way – the sea which is the home of the evil spirits."

Although Jason spent so much time in *kelod* the gods were surprisingly kind to him. It was mid-afternoon when he came in from a long session in the waves in front of his cottage. The beach was almost deserted but at the top of the sand in the shade of a casuarina tree he spotted a blonde, lily white girl in a red bikini who was sitting on a brightly coloured towel. Jason had not seen her before and he took special notice of her since single Western girls were now one of Bali's rarest commodities. He smiled at her and she gave him a wave. He then changed direction so as to go up and say hello to her.

"I was watching you ride those waves," she said. "That second to last one was amazing."

"Yes, I rather enjoyed it too. Are you a new arrival here?"

"Yes, I flew in this morning. Can't you see from my white skin that I've just come from the beginnings of the English winter? This is the first time that I've been out in the sun since August. And I'm afraid that last summer in England was not the greatest which is why I'm under the tree. I don't want to get too much sun too soon and look like a beetroot."

Jason rammed his surfboard into the sand and sat down beside her to talk. Even with her pale skin Jason thought that she looked great – so slim and graceful – and, of course, once she got a bit of a tan, she would look even better. She told him that her name was Lettie.

"That's nice; I've never met a Lettie before," he said.

"I'm not surprised. It's a most unusual name and I really don't like it very much."

"Is that the name you were christened with or is it short for something?"

"It's short for Lettice. I was named after a great-aunt who was something of a social butterfly in the 1920s. They had silly names like that in those days."

"And do you take after her? I mean, are you a party creature?"

"Yes, I like going to raves."

"So do I. And where do you live in England?"

"At Scarborough. It's a beach resort in Yorkshire."

"But that's amazing. I surf at Scarborough in Perth which is named after your Scarborough." And that was not the only amazing coincidence as Jason

130

discovered when he asked her why she came here in defiance of the Western governments' travel warnings.

"Well, I'd been saving up to come here for two years and I'd bought a pre-booked ticket on which I couldn't get a refund. After the bomb went off I couldn't decide whether or not to cancel."

"And what was it that persuaded you to come?"

"Well, I went to see my grandparents and they told me how they had been in London during the Blitz and that a single bomb was mild compared to what they had been through. Then they started talking about how Britain had a secret reserve of strength in its people and how we wouldn't have won the War if it wasn't for Churchill and all that sort of thing. Older people seem to see things in a longer light and they're not so easily swayed by television."

"Yes, I know," said an amazed Jason. "You know, Lettie, I think we've got a few things in common." Such was the start of the most beautiful relationship of Jason's life. They swam and sunbathed together, he taught her how to ride a surfboard, they sat on the beach and watched the orange sunsets and at night they ate in magical and romantic settings under the stars. Bali had given him both waves and love. And it also gave Lettie a deep, golden tan that made her more lovely than ever. The only times that Jason called her by her full name was when he wanted them to do something beautiful. "Lettice make love."

Instead of tiptoeing through life to a safe death Jason and Lettie were experiencing the power of passion and living every moment to the full. And, because of the bomb and the resulting "travel warnings", they virtually had the whole island and its waves to themselves. Out of death comes life. Out of evil comes good. They were even starting to believe in reincarnation.

WASTED WAVES

Part One

It was in the later years of the eighteenth century that the world's last and largest ocean was properly discovered and charted by great sea captains like the Englishmen, James Cook and George Vancouver, and the Frenchmen, Bougainville, La Perouse and Bruny D'Entrecasteaux. The islands of the Pacific were to be changed forever and none more so than Hawaii.

When Captain Cook stood on the deck of his ship and watched the Hawaiians riding the great waves that rolled in to the bay he was witnessing a display of skill and beauty that typified the people of the islands. Tall, athletic and pleasure loving, they revelled in such things as water sports, dancing the hula, feasting, singing and gambling.

Men and women would meet together and surf naked at the water festivals that were held on the warm, tropical beaches in an ambience of sexual freedom and lack of inhibitions. Guys and girls who rode the same wave in the natural state would be so aroused by the excitement of the ride and the beauty of their fellow surfer that sharing a wave would often lead to sharing a bed.

In the wake of the Western explorers and navigators came an altogether different species, the missionaries, with their rigid and killjoy ideas as to how the "happy savages" of the Pacific were henceforth to lead their lives.

It was in 1820 that into this world of freedom, pleasure and light stepped the forces of darkness in the form of a group of Calvinist missionaries from Boston whose twin objects were to destroy the pleasures and carefree lifestyle of the Hawaiians and to steal their land. All done in the name of the Bible, of course, and for the good of the natives.

Boston, it might be remembered, is near where the Pilgrim Fathers landed on the *Mayflower* some two hundred years earlier to wreak similar damage on the Red Indians and to infect a virus of intolerance into the American body politic that has never quite been eradicated – the witchcraft trials at Salem, Prohibition in the 1920s, the anti-smoking hysteria, political correctness and, of course, the endless and futile "war on drugs" which has imprisoned millions of young people – some of them surfers - for victimless crimes. America on a morals crusade is not a pretty sight!

The leader of these severe Calvinist bigots was Hiram Bingham who was determined to stamp out anything that made people happy. He ingratiated himself with the Hawaiian queen, Kaahumanu, (allegedly sleeping with her) and, under the force of his personality, she banned singing, dancing, gambling, alcohol, sexual freedom and surfing – in other words, all those things that make life worth living.

In order to advance his cruel and horrible programme Bingham stooped to telling lies, the most outrageous of which was that surfing was against the laws of God when, in fact, it is one of the most beautiful gifts that our Creator has given us for our health and enjoyment.

And so began the Hawaiian Dark Age which lasted for more than half a century. Like slaves on a plantation the happy and carefree islanders were pulled out of the sea by the missionaries and their agents and were made to work as labourers on the new sugar estates that just happened to be owned by – yes, you guessed - the missionaries and their families.

Because of the primitive punishments meted out by these "men of the cloth" the islanders were afraid to go into the waves with a surfboard and anyway, they were so busy working in the fields for the missionaries on low wages that there was no time for surfing or indeed any of their other traditional pleasures. And so surfing died out as a sport and the greatest waves in the world were left to break on a sterile shore.

Around the beginning of the twentieth century other – and nicer – Americans began to arrive in Hawaii. During their travels around the islands some of these observant and imaginative souls came across a surfboard or two in a museum. Their curiosity aroused, they wanted to know how the boards were ridden and what were the arts of surfing. The problem was that nobody really knew as most of the old wooden surfboards had rotted and the skills of a banned sport were hardly likely to be handed down from father to son.

These curious and water loving Americans started scouring the coastal villages of the islands to try to find old men who might be able to remember and pass on some of the things they used to do in the waves as young boys before the arrival of Mr. Bingham and his sad faced team.

Thus was surfing resurrected from its grave and the wonderful waves that travel all the way across the North Pacific to break on the Hawaiian shore were no longer to be wasted. The lost treasure had been found and man was free to surf again. Or was he?

Part Two.

We are now at a place called California Beach in the year 2020 and those dark, killjoy forces that are never far under the surface of American life have risen again.

California Beach is a fictional place on the west coast, the Pacific waves throwing themselves against its rocky point and long, sandy beach. It was the paradox of many top surfing spots – a magical wave for carefree, thrill seeking young surfers and prime real estate so expensive that it could be bought only by the well-heeled elderly. And, of course, having invested so much of their money in the place, these rich, powerful and well-connected people purchased the local council and proceeded to use it to fashion California Beach to their own liking – and that included getting rid of the surfers.

Not only did these brazen young men change into their wetsuits on the beach in full view of the public but some of their girl-friends sunbathed in only a tiny g-string! This provoked a serious outbreak of "nipplemania", with the morals brigade methodically patrolling the sand dunes in search of uncovered nipples and, upon finding a pair, giving the offender a stern dressing down and two large scallop shells to put over the offending parts.

Not surprisingly, such an invasion of personal privacy was resented by some of the girls – and their boyfriends – in robust words and so "obscene language" was added to the long list of other crimes that were laid on the surfing community.

And what about Bobby? After a two hour session in the waves, he decided to relax in a small

136

depression in the sand hills. So as not to get the sun on his face he pulled his hat down over his eyes and lay there in his swimming trunks.

The problem was that, unlike most other surfers who keep trim and healthy by eating lots of fresh fruit and vegetables, Bobby was a fast food addict who had eaten so many hormone fed chickens from the local takeaway that he had started to grow breasts.

A few minutes after he had dropped off to sleep he was spotted by the nipple brigade. Viewing his rather well developed breasts, they screamed at the sunbathing figure that she was a disgrace to her sex and would she please cover her nipples with a couple of their scallop shells.

They even got the council to pass an ordinance making it a crime for a woman to have more than 75% of her breasts exposed on the sand and everyone – men and women – could be fined $500 and spend sixty days in prison if they show more than 66% of their buttocks. [Now you, the reader, must think that I, the writer, have gone completely into the world of unreality, if not perversion; however, this mad law is taken not from imagination but from real life; they have this very law and these very penalties for its infringement in Manatee County, Florida, which, being on latitude 25°, is not the type of place where one would want too much covering in the hot sun.]

This new and zany law brought on to the sands of California Beach a whole army of council "inspectors" with their tape measures. Some of these official pervs lingered so long with the tape measure that sunbathers began to get skin rash in sensitive places. But the surfers still came to California Beach and rode the waves.

The next move of the "silvertails" was to make allegations to the police that they could smell something "funny" in the sand dunes which must be "cannabis sativa". This led to police raids where they planted drugs on several surfers who were sentenced to long periods in the state's primitive and brutal jails. But other surfers replaced them on the waves.

The streets of California Beach soon became like a Nazi camp and no surfer could drive along the main street without being pulled up and asked for ID, car registration, etc. and then a full scale search of the vehicle "for drugs" in full view of the shoppers, the surfer being spread-eagled across the bonnet of his car with a cop's gun at his head. But the surfers still came because the wave was so good.

The council then decreed that, because of "friction" between surfers and swimmers in the sea and in the interests of "safety", the surfers must surf on one side of an imaginary line with the swimmers on the other. Of course, the line was deliberately drawn to exclude the best part of the wave from the surfing zone. But the surfers still came and continued their rides over the imaginary line into the "swimmers' zone".

Then it happened. Like manna from heaven for the council and the oldies a sixteen year old surfer, who was having the ride of his life, sped over the notional line and hit a swimmer on the head, inflicting serious brain damage.

Before the injured swimmer had even reached the beach he was being pestered by five different lawyers in their swimming trunks who just happened to

138

be sunbathing with their families and who couldn't believe their good fortune that a lucrative personal injuries action should unravel before their very eyes.

Like kids at a lolly scramble, they ran and splashed around the injured man while screaming out their offers as if they were at a car auction. "I can get you ten million", and "My firm never settles for less than twenty million" and "We have professional witnesses on our books who will testify whatever we tell them".

The injuries were bad enough to require a long term of hospitalisation followed by full time care for the rest of his life. In other words, a lawyer's dream. Even though the man was insured for just such a catastrophe the lawyers and insurance company persuaded him (through his family) to sue the party that was responsible for the accident. The sixteen year old surfer? No, he didn't have any money. The local council? Well, they had tried to separate the swimmers from the surfers by their imaginary line so how could they be held responsible for the accident? But, of course, they were because they had the money or, shall we say, the means of getting it. In the eyes of the law they "had not provided proper safety in the water".

They were, in fact, insured for these sorts of things but it wasn't that simple. Nothing is in lawyer mad America. Having been forced to pay out millions of dollars to the injured man, their insurance company cancelled the premium and no other insurance company would insure them. So the next accident would have to be paid for by increasing the rates on all the expensive properties. Which is exactly what happened a few months later when a similar accident occurred.

In order to avoid any further payouts and to appease their angry ratepayers the council took the easy way out by banning all surfing at California Beach. But a few brave boys still surfed there.

The council's next move was to introduce armed security guards – some on the beach and others in inflatable motor boats so that they could make arrests in the waves, every one of which took place on the seaward side of the boat so that the public could not see the physical beating that the fat goons in uniform were dishing out to the surfer in the water.

This really did put a stop to surfing at California Beach and the residents were delighted that they had at last got rid of all the long haired surfers and their dreamy and all but naked girlfriends. The resort was now the type of place where politically correct Boston Puritans could come for their holidays without having any of their many prejudices and sensibilities violated. Hiram Bingham would have been delighted.

Other councils on the coast, wary of similar accidents, saw the surfing ban as "promoting safety in the sea and protecting the financial interests of the ratepayers" and, one by one, they emulated the trail blazers of California Beach until a whole swathe of coastline, comprising all the best surfing spots in California, was closed to surfing and every one of those wonderful waves was wasted. It was just like Hawaii during the Dark Age. And, of course, it was done "for the good of the community" and "in the interests of safety".

OF AIR AND WAVES

From an early age Chris had always had two passions – surfing and flying. The former he acquired as a kid on the Gold Coast of Queensland where he was brought up near the waves. Although of an old Australian family (free settlers and not First Fleeters!) his parents had spent much of their lives in New Guinea where they had a large coconut plantation but, like so many other "old New Guinea hands", they had returned to Australia after New Guinea embarked on the perilous road of independence in 1975 and they settled into an easy life on the Gold Coast. However, Chris's Uncle Clive had stayed on in New Guinea where he ran a one man flying boat service to and from the far flung islands that lie north-east of the main island. And it was on a holiday visit to Uncle Clive that Chris fell in love with flying boats and decided to become a pilot.

After leaving school he did a pilot's course at his local aerodrome. Then, after a short stint of a few months as a bush pilot in Australia, he went up to New Guinea and helped his ageing uncle with his business.

"Donald Duck" was a Short Sealord Mark III flying boat – a small machine that could carry seven passengers plus a load of freight that would be stuffed through the freight entrance hatch on the starboard side. With its reversible pitch propellers Chris found it easy to manoeuvre on the still waters of the lagoons where they landed.

New Guinea is a mountainous land with few roads and only primitive boat services between the main island and the smaller ones; thus aviation in its various forms provides a bigger proportion of transport than in other lands.

Over the years Clive had built up a small but regular business, ferrying passengers and goods to and from the small, inaccessible islands that were not part of the normal aviation network. However, he was getting on in years and, after acquainting Chris with the routes and business contacts, he let the keen young man do it on his own some weeks while he stayed on the ground.

Like surfing, flying gives a wonderful sense of freedom but being the pilot of a flying boat, which can be landed on any stretch of calm water anywhere on the planet, takes that freedom beyond the normal bounds. In his free time Chris would fly a few hundred miles over the islands, swooping down for a landing in the lagoon whenever he spotted waves crashing on to a beach or point. Then, once the flying boat had come to its halt, he would open the hatch, throw down his surfboard and paddle across the clear blue water to either the outer reef or the island itself where the surf would be breaking on the other side.

Some of the islands were inhabited; others were not. And, of course, whenever he landed for a surf, there was never a crowd problem. He had the Pacific to himself – as far as his eye could see. And, from the cockpit of the flying boat, his eye saw an awful lot.

Uncle Clive was a bachelor and, being relieved of so much of the work by his eager and energetic nephew, he found himself spending more and more time at the expats' club in Port Moresby where he tended to drink himself into oblivion. With the diminishing group of planters who had stayed on he would drink in one corner of the club where they would conclude that New

Guinea and indeed the world itself was going to the dogs. Well, Uncle Clive was certainly going to the dogs and, within a year of Chris's arrival, he was diagnosed with cirrhosis of the liver and he died shortly afterwards.

His only real asset was the flying boat which he left to Chris in order to keep the business going. However, when the next generation takes over a business it generally has its own ideas for change and Chris was no exception.

Having seen so much of New Guinea and the Solomon Islands from the air on clear, tropical days Chris decided that the real potential lay not in ferrying low paying passengers and freight, as had hitherto been the case, but in using the Sealord to take paying surfers to fantastic, uncrowded waves that had not been ridden before.

He knew that places like Bali and Nias and Cloudbreak in Fiji were now thick with surfers who had to fight for every wave which, of course, made surfing less pleasurable than it should be. A busy Western surfer on a fortnight's holiday didn't want to spend it fighting for waves along with every other Tom, Dick and Harry. And, by going to one spot, the surfer might strike a long, flat spell whereas on the flying boat he could be flown hundreds of miles and be put down whenever white water was seen breaking cleanly off point, reef or beach. Of course, it would not be cheap as flying boats do not run on fresh air; it took 120 gallons to fill its two tanks.

Chris started off by advertising in the Australian surf magazines for groups of seven to go on this unique surfing safari. He had so many replies that he was able to fill six slots of a fortnight each. Then word spread along the line-ups of the world and he got clients – or, as he called them, "fellow surfers" – from America, England and Europe.

Using the bay of Port Moresby as the point of embarkation, he would stuff the plane with tents, surfboards, repair kit and provisions and then rev the engine to jerk the plane forward into the head wind, its pontoons bouncing off the water. Within five seconds they would be airborne after roaring across only a hundred yards of smooth water. He would then fly his passengers across the Owen Stanley mountains and out to sea.

Ahead lay thousands of islands over which they would fly low to check out the surf and, where favourable, they would land on the lagoon since a reef and a lagoon seemed to be part and parcel of every island. If the waves were really good, they would stay a few days, camping under the casuarina and coconut trees.

Although the waves were good the pleasure and sense of freedom in being able to land wherever one fancied was even better. Since 70.8% of the planet is covered with ocean the choice of where to land was rather wide. No need to find a prepared landing ground; any bit of calm water – ocean, lagoon or lake – would do.

The experience of landing on water, leaving a long, clean trail of white foam in one's wake, turned out to be a real thrill for a generation who had only ever known planes that flew from one airport to another. The Second World War and the years immediately thereafter were the golden age of flying boats; after that they were taken out of service one by one as commercial aviation opted for more conventional planes that would go from one fixed landing ground to another. For Chris and his surfer passengers the act of spinning along the surface of the water in a flying boat was not unlike riding a surfboard on the wave.

Limited only by the weather and the availability of waves, they would fly wherever they wished – sometimes to the Solomons and even down to the New Hebrides (Vanuatu) and New Caledonia. And no matter how many surf breaks Chris found and rode he knew there were thousands more out there that were waiting to be discovered. He sometimes chuckled to himself when he thought of the crowded line-ups of Sydney, the Gold Coast, California and Hawaii

In addition to surfing Chris and the others would go skin diving among the colourful coral gardens that lay under the sea. And, of course, the ever present coconut trees gave a delicious drink when they came out of the waves or up from the coral.

At the end of a jaunt the surfers used to thank Chris and tell him how lucky he was to be cruising high over the Pacific in search of waves – and finding them – while they had to go back to their offices in Sydney, Los Angeles and London. "Not at all," he replied. "Every surfer should have a flying boat. It's a necessary part of my surfing equipment; otherwise how on earth would I get to the waves?"

CONTEST WITH A DIFFERENCE

Jerry Newcombe was an imaginative and radical surfer with a highly individual style. Because he spent so many hours in the water this radical and free thinking attitude tended to wash up on the beach and determine his behaviour on shore. In other words he paddled his own surfboard both in the waves and out of them.

This, of course, led to several brushes with Authority but it also led to him founding his own business and making a million before he was thirty.

His first brush with Authority came at the age of fourteen when he entered a surf contest and won it. Not only did he get a silver cup but also a small cheque which was enough to buy himself a new pair of boardshorts.

Thirty days later he received a letter from the national surfing association, demanding that he repay the money since he was not professional. He refused and was banned from entering competitions for a year. In the next two or three years some of his surfing buddies suffered the same fate. In fact, it seemed that the main function of the surfing association was to ban this surfer for taking a cash prize and that surfer for refusing a drug test and another surfer for getting drunk at the "after contest" party and so on. With his usual clarity of mind Jerry wondered just what the association did for the sport and came to the conclusion that surfing would be better off without it.

When he left school at sixteen he went to art school for a year and in his spare time began designing and making t-shirts which, because of their *risqué* designs, were snapped up by surfers and others.

So great was the demand that he started a small factory near the beach and got other surfers to work for him. He paid decent wages and the word soon spread that these were locally created products that were sturdy in make and stunning in design.

The concept for the t-shirt business had come to him late one night when he was sitting on the beach after a barbecue, listening to the waves. In fact, that was when most bright ideas revealed themselves with stunning clarity inside his buzzing brain.

The company had expanded from t-shirts into other surf products and was now making millions. The previous day he had had a meeting with his accountant who had advised him to splash out on some form of sponsorship which would be tax deductible.

The idea initially appealed to him as he had always hated the thought of his hard earned money being taken off him by a bunch of crooked and spendthrift politicians whose only real ability was to spend other people's money.

However, upon further reflection he couldn't think of anything that he would want to sponsor – certainly not a surf contest run by the surfing association which had banned him for a year for not putting into their coffers the pittance that he had won as a teenager.

As he sat on top of the dunes after dancing all night at the rave club he couldn't help but notice how peaceful and beautiful it all was – the beach, the waves, the warm night, the stars, the moon and the solitude. The music from the club was still resonating inside his head as he began to think of surfing in its purest and most basic form – as only a true surfer can.

He had attended several contests over the years and had noticed that, unlike a few years ago, the best surfers were no longer entering. This, he reasoned, was, like so many other problems in surfing, the fault of the surfing association and its blind adherence to the "anti-doping" hysteria which was sweeping through the sports world like an out-of-control tornado.

Jerry could understand the need to ban performance enhancing drugs in sports like athletics, weight lifting and swimming, where stamina was all that mattered, but surfing and snowboarding were different because they were sports of style rather than brute strength.

The only reason why the surfing association had fallen into line and got into bed with the anti-doping agency was because the government had made such a stance conditional on getting government grants for sport but, as Jerry reflected, the only reason why the surfing association needed a grant was to pay all the salaries and travelling expenses of its excessive number of administrators. And it was the surfers who suffered as more and more of them were forced to avoid contests because, for reasons of dignity and privacy, they were not prepared to pee into a bottle just to oblige the administrators and the weirdos at the anti-doping agency. Jerry had his own opinion about the types of people who would make their living by playing around with bottles of other people's urine. Only dogs and racehorses should be forced to have a urine test – not surfers entering a contest. The anti-doping laws were, he concluded, killing competitive surfing and, after the talk with his accountant, he decided to do something about it.

Yes, his company would sponsor a surf contest but it would be completely independent of the surfing association and the anti-doping regime. Fun and freedom instead of urine bottles and officialdom.

Never one to let the grass grow under his feet, Jerry called a media conference the next afternoon to which he invited representatives from all the surf magazines as well as the national dailies and television stations.

Seated behind a row of microphones in the conference room, Jerry lit a cigar and then made a brief statement. "In order to get back into the competitive fold all the best surfers who no longer enter contests because they refuse to humiliate themselves by passing water into bottles for the benefit of the anti-doping fanatics, my company will sponsor a surf contest – prize money a hundred thousand dollars – which will be open to all and free of the activities of both the surfing association and the anti-doping agency. We do not believe in discriminating against surfers who, because they might have had a smoke the night before, are presently prevented from entering contests. Surely such a mad situation is not in the wider interests of surfing. Any questions?"

"Yes. Does that mean that a surfer may smoke a bong on the beach and then pick up his board and run into the waves for the contest?"

"Yes. And maybe win it."

"What if one of the surfers is tripping on acid?"

"Then we should see some amazing aerials."

One thing was certain: this was going to be a contest like no other. The outcry in the media from the morals brigade, the "health and safety" fascists, the

149

police and all the sad faced "drugs counsellors" kept the issue alive in the weeks leading up to the contest with the result that Jerry's company got so much exposure that its sales – and profits – sky rocketed.

Of course, he received a threatening letter from the World Anti-Doping Agency (WADA) in Montreal which could not believe that, after all its "anti-doping" propaganda, there would be anyone on the planet who would dare to challenge its dictatorial authority. This only hardened Jerry's attitude and so he decided to throw in a triathlon as well with another huge cash prize.

By now the interest of the whole world was aroused by this new concept of pushing sport beyond the conventional bounds and sportsmen and sportswomen from all over the world, who had spent years in hard training and were now under two year bans from WADA for things like taking the wrong cough mixture or having too much caffeine, were lining up to take part.

So great was the interest that Jerry decided to auction the television rights. The price he got was somewhere in the stratosphere and so he decided to increase the prize money to a million for the surfing and another million for the triathlon. And, with part of the millions that were left over from the television rights, he bribed the local councillors to allow such an unusual event to take place on their turf.

On the day itself more than a quarter of a million spectators crowded the beach and the triathlon route to watch the action – surfers doing weird and wonderful manoeuvres on the waves and big breasted athletes achieving faster times than anything previously recorded.

The expression session was an exhibition of surfing, the likes of which had never been seen before. How could mere humans do such things? Well, quite easily in view of the nature of the contest. After this, who on earth would ever want to watch a "normal" surf contest again?

The winner of the triathlon had so much energy left over after crossing the winner's line on his bicycle that he turned around and did the whole course again.

In view of the times achieved in the triathlon there were calls from around the world for an alternative Olympic Games to be held free of the ever increasing restrictions imposed by the anti-doping regime and Jerry was hailed for taking sport into a new dimension.

For Jerry it was a "win, win, win" situation. He had brought the best surfers back into competition, he had dealt a blow to the surfing association that had used its tin-pot authority to ban him from contests when he was fourteen, he had increased his sales and pocketed more than a million from what was left over from the television rights and, by pulling the carpet from under their feet, he had exposed WADA as a tin god with no clothes on.

All around the world urine bottles were being smashed by joyous sportsmen who, at last freed from the tyranny of the anti-doping regime, were able to choose whether to enter the official contests or the "unofficial" ones. And, of course, it was in the unofficial ones where the best times were recorded and the most radical wave manoeuvres were seen. And all because a surfer had used his imagination to look beyond the narrow bounds imposed by officialdom.

ISLAND OF DESIRE

Johnny could see that the flimsy outrigger canoe was going to be smashed against the protruding mountain of coral that rose three feet out of the water so he jumped into the warm, swirling sea with his surfboard and began paddling for all he was worth.

In the brilliant light of the early morning he could see the deep blue water extending as far as the shimmering horizon. It gave him a feeling of space. A few hundred yards to the south was a small, low, palm fringed island. He was not alone; all around him were porpoises that seemed to be enjoying this part of God's ocean as much as he was.

The water was so clear that he could see right through to the bottom. It was a whole universe down there of coral gardens with branching arms in garish greens and bright blues, thin black shapes that looked like skeletons and whole trees of soft pinks, yellows and purples. Swimming among them were brilliantly coloured sea creatures. Johnny could see a giant coral fish with a dozen orange tails and a striped body like a zebra. Some of the fish were trying to hide in the coral but he could see them all. In fact, he could see everything – especially the long, liquid line of swell that was about to burst into life as a breaking wave with his name written all over it.

He paddled faster than he had ever paddled before and his surfboard was positively speeding when it and the wave connected at exactly the right moment. Suddenly all the forces of the universe united to give the surfer the ride of his life.

As his feet hit the fibreglass deck he was carried forward by forces greater than he had ever known.

Steering his board up and down and across the breaking wave with surprising ease, he saw ahead of him a great hollow tunnel of water that was about to take him inside. Into this womb of the ocean he went, drawn like a magnet. Now he was inside like a train surging through its pipe like shape on his way to the other end. The noise of the wave sounded like the roar of the train. Except that this tunnel was made by nature and not by the hands of man. And whereas the railway tunnel is for everyone, his tunnel was made for him alone.

Towards the end the sun shone through the water and he could see his god-like reflection on the wall of the wave. "I am the ocean," he thought. "We are one."

Back in the sunlight he stayed on his board and the wave carried him on and on over the submerged coral for what seemed like an eternity. It was so easy to ride this endless wave that he threw his hands up in the air and rode it shorewards like the winner of a marathon approaching the finishing line.

As soon as his feet touched the white sand of the beach he could see moving shapes coming out from behind the palm trees that fringed the beach.

His first sight was of a native girl wearing only a grass skirt, her breasts swinging as she ran down the beach to greet him. More and more people began to appear – all young, shapely and smiling.

The girls, all clad in grass skirts, began touching his fair haired god whom the ocean had delivered on to their beach as a gift for the island. First they stroked his long, golden hair, then his breasts and legs and then the rest of him. It gave him a nice feeling.

Suddenly the most beautiful creature he had ever seen emerged from the trees wearing only a bright red poinsettia. She was carrying a garland of frangipani, bougainvillea and other colourful flowers. Walking ever so gracefully, she approached Johnny and put it around his neck. Then another beauty arrived with a circlet of flowers which she placed on his head as if to crown him the king of the island.

After this coronation another maiden put a bowl of cool, fresh water into his hands. It was sweet tasting and good and he drank from it copiously. After he had finished he lay back on the warm sand and basked in the blinding sun. Everything was peaceful, mellow and pleasurable.

Suddenly he felt the soft and sensuous touch of the girl who had crowned him as she ran her tiny fingers over his chest and then down to his groin. Others followed and it seemed that their hands were everywhere; it was like being massaged by a hundred maidens, all wanting to please him. He just lay there and enjoyed it, his manhood expanding to its full extent. Could anything be better than this?

All of a sudden the peace of the island was broken by a loud noise. Like a door opening. Then he heard his mother's sharp voice, "Time to get up, Johnny. If you lie there dreaming, you'll never get to school on time."

CHAMPION OF FREEDOM

John and Margaret Gully were billed as 'Australia's most successful career couple" which was code for an awful lot of things, most of them not very nice. He was the editor of the nation's most popular tabloid while she was a Member of Parliament with eyes on one day becoming the country's first woman Prime Minister.

Despite her husband putting her photo in his paper every other day and all sorts of other publicity stunts to make the public aware of her, the Gullys were just not getting the traction that they needed to fulfil their limitless ambitions. After all, she was only one of more than a hundred M.P.s, each of whom was playing the same game of promoting themselves to the public in order to advance their careers. So, suffering from 'limelight deficiency syndrome", they came to the conclusion that something more was needed.

They paid a substantial amount of money to a leading PR firm to come up with something that would capture the hearts of Australians and establish Margaret Gully as the most wonderful woman in the land so that she could leapfrog over the backs of her colleagues to the premiership. Then, as Prime Minister, she would be able to leak to her husband's newspaper all the hot government stories so that he could get all the scoops and sell more copies of his rag. And, of course, receive a much bigger share of government advertising. He in turn would use his paper to boost his wife and smear anyone who criticised her. Their game was every bit as good as the Clintons.

When this power couple sat down with the PR guru to plot an "entirely new and revolutionary strategy" they quickly realised that he was worth every one of the thousands of dollars they had paid him.

He immediately embarked upon his patter which he had thought out beforehand and practised to perfection.

"We must work from basics," he began. "What are the Australian people most noted for? Yes, I have it. Their charity and their love of gambling. Look how generously they respond to telethons and raffles while their itch to gamble is such that, if they see two flies crawling up the wall, they'll have a flutter to see which one gets to the top first.

So, charity it must be but what kind of charity? Why, we must go with the mob and click into the current mania about child abuse. So, by a process of logical thought, we are getting there. You must start up a charity for abused children."

"But there are dozens of charities for abused children," interjected John Gully. "Why should ours be any better than the others?"

"A good point and we must deal with it. But how? Send up a prayer to the founder – indeed the god – of the PR industry."

"Who is that?"

"None other than Doctor Goebbels himself. The greatest manipulator of the public mind in the history of mankind and one to whom every PR man looks for guidance. Do you hear me, Josef? What should we do? Ah, he is hearing my prayer. It is coming to me. We must link the Australian's generosity to charity to his love of gambling. Ah yes, celebrities. That's another

156

mania of the moment. And hair. Yes, hair. By Jove, I've got it."

"Well, thank God for that," exclaimed Margaret. "Now tell us what we have to do."

"Right. You start a charity for abused children with maximum hype in the media. And, unlike any other charity in the history of our country, you will raise a hundred million dollars in only a few weeks."

"How?"

The PR guru started writing down names on his notepad. Then, when the list showed ten names, he pushed it across the table to his current clients.

At the top of the list was the Prime Minister. Then the Leader of the Opposition. Then the conductor of the national orchestra, the Lord Mayor of Sydney, Australia's top rock star, the captain of the country's cricket team, the nation's leading comedian and the World Surfing Champion, Buzz Rimmer of Narrabeen.

"Nine people and you, Margaret, make ten."

"What's this all about?"

"You announce in your tabloid that people can pledge money for each of these celebrities to shave their heads. There are ten people and, when the amount pledged gets to ten million for each person, that person is asked to shave his head and, upon doing so, the money that has been pledged against his name is then paid to the new charity.

Ten people at ten million each makes a hundred million dollars – more than has ever been raised before. The Aussies will have great fun with their flutter and you'll be seen as a brilliant innovator who is capable of solving problems. Just the type of person we need as our next Prime Minister. You notice that, apart from the

Prime Minister and the Leader of the Opposition and yourself, all the people on the list are chaps who have impressive manes of hair and the public won't be able to resist the urge to see them shave it all off."

When it was announced in John Gully's tabloid it took everyone by surprise – especially the contestants. At Question Time in Parliament the Prime Minister was asked if he would shave his skull. "Now, why would I want to do that?" he replied.

Up jumped the Leader of the Opposition. Already millions of dollars were being pledged by punters who could choose which celebrity they would back with their money. As a political statement the Opposition Leader declared that, in the interests of charity, he would shave his head upon donations for him reaching ten million dollars and was the Prime Minister such a "meany" that he would deprive abused children of so much money because, if the head was not shaved, the people who had pledged their money to that particular celebrity did not have to hand it over. Well, there could be only one answer to that. "Yes," sighed the Prime Minister, "if it is for charity. I'll do it."

The Lord Mayor of Sydney was caught in a similar bind as elections were pending and he did not want to be seen by the voters as a spoilsport who would not take part in a bit of fun for charity.

The captain of the cricket team was ordered by the cricket authorities to go along with it because they were about to ask the government for a substantial grant to promote cricket among abused children and could hardly do so without being co-operative on the hair front.

And what about the poor chap who was the conductor of the national orchestra? He had spent years growing his beautiful, brown, shoulder length hair which had become his trademark and, since it was as much a part of his body – and his image – as his arms and legs, he did not want to part with it. But Margaret Gully was on the Parliamentary committee that decided the annual grant to the orchestra and he was told that, if he would not co-operate, then he could jolly well go back to Germany and his work permit would be revoked. Since he was thoroughly enjoying living in Australia he reluctantly complied.

Margaret herself, of course, was the only woman on the list and she was the first to reach the ten million mark; the prospect of seeing a woman having her head shaved – like those women in France who collaborated with the Nazis and were shaved at the end of the war and paraded through the streets on carts as a humiliation – was simply too delicious for most people.

Before the list was published the rock star had already decided to shave his head in order to get a bit more publicity and traction in his waning career and so he merely put off his appointment at the hairdresser until the ten million was reached.

As for the comedian – he said that he was already the funniest looking man in Australia but, if he could be made to look even funnier in the interests of charity, then he would be only too happy to oblige but on condition that his clipped locks be placed on permanent display in the National Museum.

The donations rolled in and one by one these 'charity sponsors" had the razor run over their heads and hoped like hell that the hair would grow back again in the shortest possible time. After only five weeks Margaret Gully had raised ninety million dollars for her new charity and she was being hailed across the land as "a thoughtful, caring and effective operator who can get things done while the other politicians just sit around talking". All the money that the Gullys had paid to the PR man was now worth it.

And what about Buzz Rimmer? Ever since he was a young teenage surfer he had had long, blond locks that fell to way below his shoulders; in fact, his hair was his most distinctive feature and went to the very essence of his being. It was widely admired, it had grown naturally and, like his surfing ability, he regarded it as a gift from God.

He grew his hair because he wanted to and anyway it suited him. Buzz without all his hair? Well, that wouldn't be the Buzz that everyone knew and liked and admired for his awesome surfing. Furthermore, he had not been asked to take part in this silly competition; like all the other contestants he had just read about it in the tabloid where there was a photo of each "contestant" with their locks and then a computer image of their shaved head. Buzz looked at the computer image of himself and immediately decided that he never wanted to look like that – not even for a few weeks and in the interests of charity.

The ten million against his name had long since been raised and, since he was the only one who had not submitted to the razor, the figure started to mount as people thought he was cunningly holding out in order to bid up the amount. So they subscribed more in a frenzy of media backed hype. Up it zoomed to twenty million and then twenty-five. It was felt that he was just being clever, playing cat and mouse until one day he would suddenly shave it all off and so the thirty million or so pledged against his name would be handed over to the new charity. But Buzz had no thought of anything like that.

He was a surfer and not a piece of public property to be manipulated by a sleazy tabloid for the purpose of promoting the editor's wife in Parliament. Buzz had always been a strong believer in the right of the individual to make his own choices and what more personal decision could be made than how you wear your hair? Hair, he reasoned, was as important as face and physique in people's recognition of others and anyway his girlfriend and all his ex-girlfriends had said how much they enjoyed stroking his lovely hair.

Buzz just got on with his surfing and hoped it would all go away. But, of course, it didn't. After all, Margaret Gully's career was involved and, if she could not deliver 100 % of what she said she would deliver, what use would she be as a leader?

Buzz was now under more pressure than any other World Champion had ever suffered. He was vilified in the press as a mean minded, selfish and insensitive brute who put his own vanity before the needs of abused children. Gully's tabloid put his photo on its front page under the headline "Australia's worst child abuser".

Buzz had no problem with his conscience. After all, ninety million had already been raised and they would be hard pressed to spend that. If he allowed himself to be manipulated by a pushy politician on this issue, wouldn't it only encourage others to try the same thing in the future? He would no longer be his own

161

master but an item of public property to be exploited by others with their own agendas.

The amount pledged against his name rose to thirty-five million and every time he went for a surf the media would harass him on the beach, sometimes even paddling out to the line-up, to ask him when he was going to shave his head "for charity". He had always thought that he lived in a free country but was beginning to have his doubts. The herd instinct seemed to prevail – especially when the word "charity" was involved. And he was very angry at the way he had been forced into such a difficult position by forces that were beyond his control.

An attempt was made by a bunch of "charity terrorists" to attack him on the beach with a battery powered razor but he and his friends beat them off, leaving the one holding the razor with a broken jaw. This unleashed a wave of tabloid hatred against both Buzz and the surfing community in general which was described as "selfish" and "a blot on Australia's reputation for kindness".

Because of this and similar attempts to get close enough to his head to shave it "for thirty-five million" the World Champion found that he could not go out without the protection of other surfers around him – like bodyguards. And, of course, there were endless abusive phone calls from what he called "charity nuts".

"How can you deprive abused children of thirty-five million just for your own selfishness?" Easy. It had something to do with individual rights. And they were not on sale for thirty-five million or indeed any other amount.

However, the public soon began to see through the tabloid fuelled campaign against Buzz and the surfing community and they began to write letters to newspapers and ring up talkback shows supporting Buzz in his stand to "do his own thing in his own way and not to be manipulated by others for their own purposes".

The polite section of the population were outraged that a grotty tabloid would take it upon itself to announce such a "competition" without having the manners to inform those who were expected to have their heads shaved. These people did not like the new culture of disrespect for the individual as manifested by such things as telemarketers disturbing the peace of the home, the increasingly nosy nature of questions on the census form, the intrusive reporting of people's private lives by the media and the requirement on filling out forms to provide all sorts of private and unnecessary information which is then put on computer for thousands of people to see. Their sympathies were entirely with Buzz.

Orchestra audiences were missing their handsome conductor with his fine locks while the comedian now looked like the town thug and nobody would ever again be able to take him seriously as a comedian.

The conservatives also came down on the side of the radical, long haired surfer on the grounds that change – even to a hairstyle – should be made democratically and not be "imposed from above by a manipulative dictatorship". In short, the people of Australia decided that they would not be comfortable in a society where people no longer had the right to decide their own personal appearance.

This led the debate into a lot of other areas where individual choice had been eroded in recent years and some of these issues were revisited and reversed. By insisting on his right to make his own decisions Buzz had caused a seismic shift in how people viewed their rights.

When asked about all this during an interview after he won the next contest he stood up to his full height, stroked his hand through his shining locks and said, "All I did was to stand up for my rights. It's no more than any surfer would do." Some surfers agreed with him, others didn't. Some saw him as a hero, others thought he was a rotter. After all, all that he had to do was to shave off his beautiful locks and abused children would have received $35 million but that would have been a violation of one of his most basic and personal rights and that, he decided, was worth more than $35 million dollars. In fact, it was worth more than all the money in the world.

WRONG TIME, WRONG PLACE

Every surfer knows what it's like to be in the wrong place at the wrong time. It might mean that, not being in the right take-off position, you miss the wave. Or that you have to jump out a top floor window when the master of the house arrives home when you are in bed with his lady. Or that you don't have any money in your pocket when a departing surfer finds that his baggage is overweight at the airport and offers to sell you his brand new surfboard for forty dollars. For Joe, being in the wrong place at the wrong time led to the biggest wipeout of all. Or so it seemed.

Joe was one of California's top surfers – a thrill seeker, a fun lover and a party animal who thought nothing of spending all night at a rave and then, wide eyed and dangerous, paddling out for the dawn session at his local beach, San Clemente. Youth, energy, virility and fun.

Reckless, rugged and answerable to nobody but himself, he always sought to get the most out of life – on his Harley, on his surfboard and by other means. In a tightly controlled, technological world Joe was one who paddled his own canoe and worried about the consequences later.

One of these was that he had been caught with a bag of Humboldt weed for which he was fined $3,000 and given a suspended prison sentence even though nobody was harmed by what he did. The only harm inflicted was by the court.

A year later, as he was riding his powerful Harley on the Santa Monica freeway, he was pulled up by a couple of cops for exceeding the artificially low speed limit by five miles an hour. Jealous of his shiny, black machine, they gave him a rough and violent body search that turned up one roach in the pocket of his jeans. Not having enough cash on him to pay the bribe that they demanded, he was then subjected to the usual treatment.

On their two-way radio they checked his "previous" and, realising that a mere roach might not be enough to separate him from his Harley by a prison sentence, they planted on him a full bag of Acapulco Gold with the result that he was out of the water for a year as he joined more than a million others in the "Land of the Free" who were languishing behind bars for committing victimless drug crimes.

To-night there was to be a rock concert on the sand near Trestles and Joe paid a mid morning visit to his friend, Shane, who lived not far from the beach at San Clemente. He had more than a thousand dollars in his pocket as, after visiting Shane, he was going to pay some bills and then go down to the beach and buy some tickets for the concert for himself and his friends. It was a night to look forward to.

Earlier in the day Shane had taken delivery of a couple of hundred grams of a certain Colombian product. When Joe walked in Shane laid out a couple of lines on top of Surfer magazine which was lying on the coffee table. Joe extracted from his pocket a crisp, new hundred dollar note which he rolled up to use.

Suddenly there was a large bang as the door was smashed down and a posse of cops and their DEA sidekicks came bursting into the room. What was going to be a rush of pleasure had turned into a horror movie. A case of being in the wrong place at the wrong time.

166

Roughly - indeed violently - the cops searched both the surfers, finding the coke on Shane and the money on Joe. In the unsophisticated mind of the law that meant one of two things - either Joe was the purchaser who was about to hand over a thousand dollars for the stuff or he was the seller who had just been paid for it.

The cops took Joe's driver's licence from his wallet and were about to radio through to the state's Orwellian computer for more details when the bedroom door opened. Shane's beautiful girlfriend, Mary Jane, stood there drowsy and naked as she groggily asked what it was that had woken her from her deep sleep.

Suddenly all the attention was switched to this luscious lady who was then pinned down on her bed by the coarse and randy drug cops. Seeing that all eyes were momentarily on Mary Jane and believing that such a chance would not recur, Joe slipped quietly out the open door, down the stairs and on to his motor bike which he rode straight to the office of Scott, who was both a fellow surfer and a lawyer.

"Mr. Torrens is busy at present," said the snooty secretary as she looked disapprovingly at this long haired surfer who was wearing only a pair of boardshorts and a torn t-shirt. "Do you have an appointment?'

Joe pushed past her towards Scott's office and entered after he had knocked. Scott was on the phone but gestured to his friend to sit down. A couple of minutes later he put down the receiver and asked Joe, "What the hell is the matter?"

"I was in the wrong place at the wrong time," said Joe as he related the events of the morning to his buddy.

"So they got your driver's licence," said Scott with a sigh. "Therefore they know who you are and where you live. My guess is that by now they are already bashing down your door, smashing your surfboard and cutting the legs and arms off your wetsuit. That's the usual drill they reserve for surfers. I've defended many of them on these ridiculous charges and it always seems to be the same. Any excuse to separate a surfer from his gear. You've had some previous trouble, haven't you?"

"Yes, twice before. The last time they planted it on me."

"So this is the third one?" asked an increasingly agitated Scott.

"Afraid so."

"That brings into play the 'three strikes and you're out' rule."

"And what's the penalty for that?"

"A minimum of twenty-five years behind bars and a maximum of life imprisonment."

"So what should I do?" gasped Joe who was beginning to think that he might have surfed his last wave.

"There's a coffee bar downstairs at the back of the building. Well hidden. We'll go down there for a talk."

"Why?"

"Because the advice I'm going to give you is not the advice I would give to a client but to a friend. Better to do it out of the office."

After ordering coffee and a couple of blueberry muffins they took the table in the corner and started talking quietly.

"There's nothing I can do to get you off this charge," said Scott. "There are thousands of people rotting away in prison for the rest of their lives for committing three minor offences – mostly drug related. The so-called 'drug war' just happens to be the current hysteria that is sweeping America. It seems that our sanctimonious nation is never happier than when it is persecuting some group who dares to be different. Once a jury hears the word 'drug' they are ready to convict without hearing any further evidence. That's how the public mind has been programmed. In Holland and other countries of Europe you wouldn't even get a conviction for any of these so-called offences but sadly our brash, new society in the States lacks the balance, tolerance and maturity of older lands."

"So I should go there?"

"Yes, but it's not as easy as it sounds. If you do a runner, which is the only sensible thing in the circumstances, the DEA will hound you to the ends of the earth and you'll never be a free man. They will get Interpol on the job and, if you try to cross a border, you'll be caught and dragged back here and be locked away forever."

"But I haven't done anything wrong. I'm not a terrorist and I've never hurt anybody in my whole life."

"You and I know that but we live in a country where a man can be sentenced to life imprisonment for having ten dollars worth of cocaine while a shopkeeper who shoots a shoplifter dead isn't even charged with an offence. You must flee immediately and, if you don't want to be caught for the rest of your life, you must get a new identity. Legally."

"How? I don't have any money; the Harley is my sole asset."

Scott lowered his voice and told him what to do.

"France?"

"Yes."

"How long?"

"Years?"

"I'm afraid it's the only way. And, don't worry, they won't ask any questions. They've been doing this for a couple of centuries. And don't contact me until you have your new identity as I don't want to be involved. Then one day, when I get a letter from France from a name that I don't recognise, I'll think back to this conversation and how I helped one nice, young chap escape from the tyranny of the American justice system."

"That's a strange thing for a lawyer to say."

"I've done too many cases to have any illusions about the 'good, ol' U. S. of A'. Unfortunately, America has too many laws and not enough justice. The state just can not keep its nose out of other people's private lives. Do you need any money?"

"Just for petrol. I had more than a thousand bucks on me this morning but the pigs took the lot."

"Yes, and they'll keep it for themselves. I've never come across an honest drug cop. Here's a couple of hundred." Scott took out his wallet and handed over the money. "Just remember, Joe, no good-byes to anyone and no contact either. Nothing less than your future freedom depends on it. Oh, and I hope you find some good waves although I hear that the Med is more for yachts than surfboards."

They shook hands and said good-bye. Scott then turned round with one final message. "Treat the whole thing as an adventure. That way it won't seem so bad. It might even be fun."

As Scott walked up the stairs to his office he heard the noise of the Harley as Joe rode to the bank to get his passport out of the "safe custody" deposit. As Scott said, it would probably be good for another few days until the slow, bureaucratic wheels of Interpol put him on computers around the world. Then, steering clear of the beach where he thought the cops might be looking for him, he rode south down the San Diego freeway, keeping well within the speed limit so as not to attract attention.

He got past the checkpoint at Camp Pendleton as the guards were stopping only northbound traffic in their search for illegal immigrants from Mexico. Past the signs for Oceanside, Carlsbad, Encinitas, Solana Beach, Del Mar, La Jolla, Downtown San Diego, Chula Vista and on to the border. Since no general alert had been put out for him yet he got across the frontier without any trouble and then inhaled the sweet smell of the freedom and disorder of Mexico.

At Tijuana he stopped for a cold drink and then rode on towards Mexico City, the dust bowl megapolis that had been founded by Cortes on the ruins of the old Aztec capital, Tenochtitlan. On the outskirts of the city he parted with some of Scott's dollars in exchange for a room at a cheap hotel. Already he was missing the waves but he knew that he was on a mission which would one day lead him back into the surf as a free man with a new identity.

After waking up late the next morning he visited some motor cycle dealers and sold the Harley to the one that offered him the best price. Then he went to the airline office and booked a flight to Paris. His next call was at a clothes shop to buy some more respectable gear than the boardshorts and t-shirt that he had been wearing ever since getting up on the morning that changed his life.

After landing at Paris Joe took the TGV train to Marseilles, disembarking in the early evening. Later that night he sat in a bar down in the Old Port and did some thinking. Should he really do what Scott suggested or should he hang out in France, surfing and having a good time? He still had a bit of money left over from the sale of the Harley. Although Scott's idea had its drawbacks it would be wise to follow it. And, as a result of being in the wrong place at the wrong time, Joe had had a crash course in "wisdom".

Thus it was that at dusk the next day he presented himself at the main gate of the military camp of the Légion Etrangère at Aubagne, a few miles from Marseilles. The wild, thrill seeking, reckless wave rider of San Clemente was about to join the French Foreign Legion, that unique military force with its unrivalled aura of romance, mystery and heroism.

Joe had bought a Petit Larousse French dictionary in Paris and had been practising his words, drawing on what he could remember from French classes at high school.

The tough looking soldier at the gate took one look at his long hair and appeared to sneer. Then, in a Lowland Scottish accent, he declared, "My hair was longer than that when I arrived here. Coom in and I'll present ye to the sergeant for new recruits."

The sergeant for new recruits was a tall, fair haired New Zealander. "So why do you want to join?" he asked Joe. "For a bit of excitement or to escape something terrible – like a nagging wife, door knocking creditors or the police?"

Scott had told him to be truthful so he said, "The police."

Without batting an eyelid the sergeant said, "We are getting more and more young Americans who are fleeing from their authorities. Most of them turn into good soldiers. And, after living in Europe and serving in Africa, none of them ever wants to go back to the States. America's loss is the Legion's gain. You do realise how tough the basic training is? Four months of sheer hell. If you can survive that, you can survive anything. It's up to you."

Following Scott's advice to treat the whole thing as an adventure, Joe pushed himself to the utmost and, after a few weeks, he received his treasured *képi*, the white cap that distinguishes a legionnaire from everyone else in the world.

Aubagne, with its Monument to the Dead, a giant bronze globe guarded at each corner by four bronzed figures of legionnaires, was the town of the Legion and, when Joe eventually got some leave, he spent it with his new friends drinking jugs of red wine in the bars around the market square, singing the Legion anthem *Le Boudin*, and chatting up all the spunky looking girls who came to Aubagne to meet the legionnaires in much the same way that their Californian counterparts came to San Clemente to meet the surfers.

Upon completing his basic training Joe was sent to Corsica to train with the airborne unit and then to the jungle training unit in French Guiana at the top of South America. His wild, risk taking nature had not been tamed; instead it had been harnessed to fit the needs of one of the world's top fighting units where daring and fearlessness were certainly not disadvantages.

After Guiana he went to West Africa to fight in a couple of the post-colonial wars that seem to have been taking place there ever since the British and the French handed their colonies back to the natives in the 1960s. Then it was back to Aubagne for a refresher course. By now he had been given his French passport under a new name which he could use legally for the rest of his life so long as he did not return to the United States which he didn't want to anyway.

At the end of the refresher course Joe, together with forty others, was chosen for an operation that was not being carried out by the Legion for political reasons but would nevertheless go ahead with legionnaires acting outside the Legion. The Comoros were mentioned - those islands between Madagascar and East Africa which, since receiving their independence from France, have had more than twenty coups d'etat.

The long and the short of it was that the recently deposed leader wanted the islands back and, during his presidency, he had transferred enough foreign aid money into his private Swiss bank account to be able to make it happen. He believed that he could place more reliance on well-trained Legionnaires than on the local soldiers in the Comoros whom he knew from experience would run away at the first sound of gunfire.

The Foreign Legion could not do it officially because the French government had recognised the new regime. Therefore the Legion gave indefinite leave of absence to Joe and the others and enough funds to get to Madagascar, a remote corner of which had been chosen as the take-off point for the invasion. "Treat it as an adventure," said Scott. Joe now knew what he meant.

From Paris they flew to Madagascar where, at the designated spot in the remote north of the island, they found the launches that had been specially chartered by the fat dictator in Paris to ferry them to the Comoros. The launches were loaded with weapons, ammunition and some small inflatable boats that would be used to take them ashore in the pre-dawn landing. Besides Joe and his group from Aubagne there were another hundred and sixty who had been given similar leave from the Legion in different parts of Africa and who had made their way in sixes and sevens to the stifling hot assembly point. Shades of D-Day!

Their orders were to capture the government buildings and installations of Moroni, the small town on Grande Comore that was the "capital" and then the rest of these far flung islands would fall like a house of cards so that the fat dictator could come back and rob his people again.

The surprise landing on the town's foreshore at 3 a.m. was unopposed and Joe and some others made their way straight to the presidential palace on the hill. After overpowering the dozy guards on the gate, they barged their way into the dark building in search of the current dictator. In the dim light of the vestibule they saw him coming down the staircase in his leopard skin pyjamas to see what all the fuss was about.

When he was ordered to surrender, a couple of shots were fired at the legionnaires by his henchmen and a good old presidential palace shoot-out ensued during which the dictator and three of his guards were killed and a legionnaire was shot in the arm.

By dawn it was all over. Besides the presidential palace the legionnaires were in control of the police station, government buildings, the radio station and the airport where they had installed one of their own as the Controller of Air Traffic. A nice little counter-coup with minimal loss of life.

While the officer in charge of the operation set himself up in the presidential palace Joe and the others took over the Hotel de la Mer, a three storey, wooden colonial style building with wide, shaded verandahs around its four sides. And they were never short of drink because up at the palace the soldiers had uncovered more than a thousand crates of champagne since expensive liquor is always the second item (after weapons) on a dictator's shopping list. The commanding officer took what he wanted and the rest of the stash was taken down to the Hotel de la Mer as and when it was needed.

Joe and his friends stretched out on the cane chairs on the big verandah which overlooked the sea. It was kept relatively cool by the palm mat awnings that waved gently in the light breeze. The soldiers had their cold drinks served to them by white coated barmen while the hotel's "good time" girls massaged their shoulders and legs and sat on their laps.

From his cane lounge chair Joe looked down on the ocean and, more particularly, the big, well-shaped waves that were rolling in and breaking over the point at the end of the town. Nobody was riding them. Perhaps, he thought, this was one of the last frontiers that surfers haven't reached. Not only was it hard for travellers to get to the Comoros but anyone who made it was likely to get caught up in a coup. This, he decided, was going to be a military occupation to remember. He hoped it would last a long time.

This was also the feeling of the officer up in the presidential palace. He sent a message by radio to the fat dictator in Paris asking for "some more money until you return but the military situation is such that a return at present would not be possible".

The dictator knew that he had no choice but to pay up as his return to the presidential palace depended on the soldiers. When the troops were asked by the commanding officer to write down their requirements, which would be flown in from Paris and Johannesburg, Joe put down for a surfboard and even provided the preferred measurements.

It arrived the following week and so it was that a very happy surfer got a chauffeur to drive him the few yards along the beach to the point for a long awaited surf in the warm waters of the Indian Ocean. The waves were clean, big and glassy and he had them all to himself. Back at San Clemente there would have been fifty surfers in the line-up.

Paddling out from the point, he reached the take-off area in no time. He cast a glance at the island; on top of the small hill was the gleaming white presidential palace and further down he could see the low buildings of the town interspersed with palm trees and other vegetation. On the top verandah of his waterfront hotel he could see his fellow legionnaires looking out through binoculars at their mad colleague who had exchanged his gun for a surfboard or, as Joe explained, "one gun for another". With so many critical eyes upon him he was determined not to disappoint them.

Out of practice he wobbled a bit to begin with but then got a truly magical ride that carried him across the wave for more than a hundred yards. There was coral underneath the sea which held the waves up for an incredibly long time.

He was enjoying it and so were the spectators – not just the legionnaires on the verandah but also the locals who had gathered on the beach to cheer this apparent god who was speeding across the top of the water like a flying boat. This only spurred him on to greater efforts and he gave them a display of boardriding that none would ever forget.

He eventually came out of the water not because he was cold, as would have been the case in California but because he was tired and his arms were beginning to ache from all the vigorous paddling. On the beach he sat down on the warm sand to dry off. The locals came up and started talking to him in French which, after so long in the Legion, he could speak reasonably well. One of the young girls started stroking him and he relaxed under the gentle and sensuous touch of her tiny massaging fingers. He took her back to the hotel with him.

It was hot on the verandah of the Hotel de la Mer so she picked up a fan made of palm leaves and started to wave it in front of his face. Other legionnaires were being fanned by other young ladies. This is how all surfs should end, thought Joe.

Since the islanders had got used to accepting whatever regime they woke up to the legionnaires found that their garrison duties were both minimal and easy

178

But the situation was still far too "dangerous" for the fat dictator to return.

Joe surfed every morning before the onshore wind started to blow. He found that the point break was a particularly powerful wave that served up a veritable feast of big, hollow tubes one after the other. Any surfer's dream.

Up at the palace the commander was also enjoying the delights of the island and, after receiving what the fat dictator declared was the last payment he could afford, he sent a message to Paris informing the hopeful tyrant of the latest "situation" which was that the legionnaires were in full control of the place and were enjoying it so much that they had no intention of handing it back to the tyrant who had paid them to go here. After all, where else could a young man live such a good life? Joe agreed.

He was the only one who surfed, the others filling in the long, languid days by swimming, skin diving or just kicking a football around on the esplanade with the friendly and obliging locals. And, unlike in San Clemente, the police were no problem; they took their orders from the legionnaires!

The Legion had not only taught him how to speak a new and beautiful language but had also opened his mind to the world with all its infinite variety in a way that would never have happened had he stayed at his local beach in California. His fellow legionnaires were a unique breed, drawn from different backgrounds and different countries. Joe had made some of the most meaningful friendships of his life since donning his képi. And he had tested himself in battle to the satisfaction of both himself and his commanding officer. As Scott said it had turned out to be an adventure.

He continued to ride those wonderful waves but no longer on his own; he had introduced some of the other legionnaires to the pleasures of surfing and they now formed a select band within the Legion. And out there in the line-up with his friends he sometimes had time for thinking and reflecting on his change in fortune. Not only was he surfing his own magical break but for ever more he would have the best line for impressing girls. "Yes, I'm a surfer. Oh, and I also served with the Legion." A party stopper in any language. The ultimate combination. Glamour. Romance. Style. Far better than being a brain surgeon or the President of the United States. The only problem was that he could never decide whether he had been in the wrong place at the wrong time or the right place at the right time.

SURFERS' REUNION

It was going to be a surfing holiday like no other for it was two years since the crew had last gathered. They had been students together at the University of Plymouth which, being ideally situated near some of Britain's best surf breaks, is the university of choice of countless surfers who like to combine their studies with the waves. *Mens sana in corpore sano* and all that sort of thing.

After graduating, the five chums had gone their separate ways – Ray had become an industrial scientist in Bristol, Ross had applied his degree in marine biology by working for an environmental trust in the Scottish Highlands, Daniel was the editor of a music magazine, Dave had gone "into finance" while Tripper had spent much of his time travelling to warm places to surf; he always seemed to be on a trip of one kind or another.

Although they had surfed together almost every day as students they now kept in touch only by the occasional e-mail or phone call; things like employment and geography had wreaked their havoc.

They all agreed that "something must be done about it" and the result was that, at Dave's suggestion, they decided to rent a house near the beach at Biarritz in south-west France where they could all gather with surfboards, girlfriends and musical instruments for a fortnight of waves, sun and fun. The whole idea was to try to "take up from where we left off" and to recreate those magic days of yesteryear.

This is always a tricky exercise for it assumes that nobody has changed. However, by the end of the first night it seemed that they had pulled it off. Only four

181

of them had arrived but by the end of an evening of wine, smoke and song it was as if the last two years had not happened. And the next day the waves were pumping as they ran into the Atlantic with their fibreglass sticks just as they did in their carefree university days. This was going to be one cruisy and mellow time.

The one who arrived last was Dave who had to fly in from Chicago where he was now based in a multi-national firm that dealt in futures. He had spent his first year out of university in a bank in the City of London where he became something of a whizz kid which led to him scoring what he claimed was a "Number One job" in Chicago. The others couldn't wait to see him again for, with his boundless energy and rather reckless attitude to life, he had always been the best of company.

Dave was an obsessive character. He started off as a skateboarder and bought all the clothes to look the part. Then, after becoming a surfer, he threw out all his skateboard clothes and wore nothing but bleached jeans, white t-shirt, sunglasses and flip flops on his feet – even at midnight in a dimly lit disco.

Then, one week-end he went to London to see a band play at Wembley and came back the full punk – the spiked, coloured hair, the body piercing, the leather, the lot. After tiring of that he went back to the surfing look but, as he said, the urban surfer and not the hippy surfer Plymouth and not Saint Agnes. However, through all these mutations he was always the life of the party, the fount of energy and a damned good surfer.

Dave did not arrive until the evening of the second day. The others drove to Biarritz Airport to meet him on his flight from Paris. He arrived complete with wo new surfboards, two wetsuits (a steamer and a spring suit), three legropes and all sorts of high tech gadgets – mostly to do with communications.

"Hi, guys," he called out as he saw them in the terminal. "You don't know how lucky you are that I got here; I nearly didn't make it because of this huge wheat contract that I had to seal only five minutes before catching the plane at Chicago. You don't know what it's like to be under pressure when millions of dollars are at stake. It's like the rush of going over the falls at Waimea several times a day." At that moment the mobile phone, that was hanging from his black leather belt, began to ring.

Dave picked it up and said "Hello". He then listened to what the voice at the other end was saying. And then he spoke. But not in a voice that any of his friends could recognise. It was the full mid-Western accent as he raved on about some cattle futures contract in the millions.

All the way back in the car Dave kept saying that he was going to hit the waves at the crack of dawn since, with Chicago being right in the heart of the North American continent, he had not seen the sea for a full year. "Just surf videos, man," he said. "I've seen every one of them. Mind you, I work six days a week and sometimes go in on Sundays too. But now is holiday and I am going to surf non-stop to make up for all the months I've been out of the water. You'll never see me in the house. Only in the waves."

"That's where we all want to be," said Ross. "Let's hope there'll be surf every day."

"There has to be; this is my holiday. You've no idea how much money I could be making at my desk right now. If there are no waves, I would have wasted my time coming here."

That evening there seemed to be a tension in the air that had not been present the night before. Daniel's girlfriend, Samantha, said that she thought that their friend had "problems". The others put it down to the stress of being on planes for so many hours.

They tried to relax him by offering him some wine and some smoke, both of which he declined on the grounds that it was now business hours in Chicago and he might receive an important phone call involving millions of dollars worth of futures and so he had to keep a sober head and clear mind at all times.

The jet lagged traveller slept soundly but woke up at 4 a.m. on account of his body clock still being on Chicago time. He got up and made a cup of coffee. Then, when the first light of dawn peeked through the night sky, he walked across the road to the beach in order to check the waves. In the early light of the new day he could see that the Bay of Biscay was as flat as a French crepe.

Back at the house he banged several doors and kicked two chairs off the balcony. "What the hell's going on?" asked a groggy Ray. "I was dreaming that was on a tropical island with a slippery mermaid and all of a sudden the Battle of the Somme breaks out."

"There are no waves," screamed Dave. "And I've flown five thousand miles to have a surf."

"You can't just turn the waves on and off like a light switch," said Tripper. "It's something to do with nature. Last year I went to Peru to surf and it was flat almost every day so I just had to chill out with Charlie and the locals. It can happen, you know."

184

"Okay, maybe I'm still a bit too zonked for a full-on surf session but, if there are no waves to-morrow, there's going to be serious trouble."

"Just calm down and be thankful that we're all together again. It's not every group of surfers that can meet up two years later for a reunion."

"Yes," said Tripper. "Last year I used to go surfing with an Australian friend in Bali but I'll never see him again."

"Why not?"

"Because he got eaten by a shark."

"Yeah, but he would have had life insurance," said Dave. "I'm insured for a couple of mill."

The others spent the day sunbathing on the lawn, talking of old times, laughing and listening to music while the girls went shopping. From the middle of the afternoon Dave spent long periods on the phone as it was another business day in Chicago. "Can you turn that music down?" he kept saying. "I don't think you have any idea how important this phone call is."

"I definitely preferred him when he was a punk," declared Daniel. "Even when he was a chundering punk."

"To-morrow there just has to be surf," screamed Dave as he went to go to bed. "It's just not possible for someone to travel all this way and not get waves."

"I'm afraid you're mistaken," said Jean-Francois, a local surfer whom they had met on the beach and who was hanging with them.

"Why?"

"Because a contest is starting to-morrow and Biarritz will get its usual contest surf."

"And what's that?"

"No bloody surf at all. Just a paddling race around the buoy at the Grande Plage to give the contestants something to do and to get their boards wet."

"Nonsense," yelled Dave. "If they've gone to all the expense of putting on a contest, there just has to be surf."

"We'll see."

More bangs the next morning when Dave found that, unlike the futures market which could be manipulated by man, the ocean had a mind of its own and not even all the wealth of the world could produce one tiny wave.

However, all was not lost and towards the end of the day some small waves began to form and it seemed that every surfer in Biarritz was out there riding them including Dave. Only problem was that it was once again business hours in Chicago and so, before going in the water, he extracted from his suitcase a waterproof mobile phone that he put into a specially made pocket of his spring suit.

Dave got his first ride for a year on a tiny swell of water that broke at about two feet. He managed to stand up on his board and ride it for a few yards until the board lost all power and he was dropped into the sea. He then rode a few more, dropping in on other surfers on the grounds that his time in the surf was more precious than theirs.

Back in the crowded line-up he started paddling to catch another small wave. However, just as he was about to take off on it his phone rang and so he kicked out and paddled to a piece of flat ocean (not very difficult!) to unzip the compartment in the leg of his spring suit so as to take the call. And it was from this

186

position in the outer part of the line-up that he gave directions for clinching yet another futures contract in Chicago.

The rest of the line-up just shook their heads. A young French surfer asked Ray if they were making a film of the session. "No. Why?" asked Ray.

"Because such a thing could only happen in a movie."

Back on the beach Ray declared that Dave was fast becoming an embarrassment but Tripper replied that, since it was all in the sphere of surreality, it was the best entertainment he'd seen since the Monkey Dance in Bali.

The next day was as Jean-Francois predicted and so was the next. "I tell you," screamed an increasingly distraught Dave, "I've seen bigger surf in Lake Michigan on a Sunday afternoon than you get in this goddammed dump. Whose idea was it to come here?"

"Yours!" they all shouted.

"Well, if I wake up again to-morrow and there's still no surf, I'm going to do something about it."

"The power of one," laughed Ross.

Again no surf. Dave disappeared during the morning, arriving back at lunch time with a string of airline tickets. He then started packing his bags. "If the waves won't come to Dave, then Dave must go to the waves," he declared. "I'm flying to Paris this afternoon and then catching a plane to Lisbon. I've looked at the weather map and there just has to be surf off the Portuguese coast. Anyone coming with me?"

"Nah, we're on holiday. Too lazy to move."

"Couch potatoes, the lot of you."

After the nervous bundle of stress departed there was a noticeable change in atmosphere – not just in the house but meteorologically speaking as well; the next morning they were woken up by a mighty noise. Not banging doors and chairs being kicked over but the thunder like sound of great waves that were rolling in from the ocean to provide the surfers of Biarritz with their best swell in months.

The morning session was like no other; powerful and beautifully formed barrels breaking with monotonous regularity. "It's days like this when you just thank God to be alive," called out Daniel as he came up from the briny after doing the floater of his life. They surfed until the muscles of their arms and legs were aching from all the paddling and being tossed about in the swirling sea.

It was while they were having a big after-surf lunch that the phone rang. It was Dave. "Guess what?" he cried into the phone.

"You got the barrel of your life?"

"No, there are no bloody waves. Just like Biarritz."

"No, not like Biarritz. We've had the best and biggest waves since that day at Constantine Bay just before the exams. Remember?"

"You're kidding."

"No. I'll take the phone outside and hold the receiver up so that you can hear the roar of the surf." He did. And poor Dave very nearly had a breakdown. "Okay, I'll come straight back. I'll try to get there by to-night but I have to come through Paris; there are no direct flights."

Unfortunately, being the height of the holiday season, there were not any spare seats either and it was three days before Dave was able to rejoin his mates. And by then the great swell had ended and the sea around Biarritz was once again as calm as a millpond.

That night they turned on the television to watch the news. It was the usual stuff – a tornado in the mid-West, another train strike in France, Israeli soldiers killing more Palestinian women and children and an eighty-five year old great-grandmother who had just had a baby after taking a new fertility pill. Then at the end was a short item stating that there had been a summer cyclone off Portugal which had produced huge waves which were "a threat to sea-walls and embankments but a boon to Lisbon's surfers who could be excused for thinking that they were in Hawaii." There was some footage of a point break with great waves that were being ridden by "surfers of skill and daring".

"My God!" screamed Dave. "That's the very point at Cascais where I was staying. I was in that hotel at the right of the picture and, if I hadn't come back to this hellhole, I would be out there catching that very wave."

"So, you haven't been very lucky?" said Ross.

"No, but I'm thinking of suing the travel agent. I told him the reason I was going to Lisbon was to surf. The thieving scoundrel took my money but didn't perform his part of the deal. There was no bloody surf. On my first day back in Chicago I'll call on my lawyer to see if anything can be done. No, it'll have to be the second day."

"Why? Have you got a prior engagement?"

"Yes, it's a weekly appointment."

"Is she a blonde or a brunette?"

"Oh, come off it, guys. It's with my psychiatrist. He's a forty-one year old balding Yank who always had a cigar in his mouth."

"Well, I guess that's a new species," declared Ross. "A surfer who goes to the psychiatrist. Most of us are kept sane by the waves."

Dave's phone rang again so he rushed into his room to answer it. "The problem as I see it," said Ray, "is that he is paddling against the wave. That's why he's not scoring any rides. There has to be harmony between the surfer, the board and the wave. Dave's so stressed out that nothing works for him any longer. The ocean gives us waves and pleasure but in return it deserves respect. It doesn't like to be screamed at by mad people who lie on the psychiatrist's couch. He should stay on the beach."

"Isn't that what he's been doing ever since he arrived?"

"It is," declared a pensive Tripper, "the ocean's way of dealing with him. In the East they call it karma."

PUFFIN ISLAND

If genes are anything to go by, then Finn McNeil was destined to be a sea creature. This fair haired, blue eyed descendant of the Vikings had been brought up on a small island off the west coast of Scotland where his father was a fisherman – at least until he was forbidden to fish in his ancestral waters by some directive of the European Union, a new and temporary organisation that was heartily detested by everyone on the island.

This rich and valuable section of Britain's fishing grounds had been surrendered to a Spanish fishing fleet by the bureaucrats in Brussels and, since there was no other industry on the island, Finn's father had been reduced to dependency on the state which was not all that different from the condition of the serfs who were his ancestors in the days of feudalism.

Having been made permanently unemployed by the E.U., Mr. McNeil began building boats. The first one was a clinker built sailing boat that he gave to Finn on his twelfth birthday. He then made a couple of larger ones which he sold for "cash under the table" to a Glasgow businessman who spent his week-ends sailing around the western isles.

Finn learned the skills of seamanship and navigation from his father and sailed his small boat around the island – sometimes to remote coves that, because of the high, rocky cliffs, could not be reached by land.

Some of the coves on the western side of the island were blessed with clean, powerful waves that were born far out in the North Atlantic and it wasn't long before Finn and the only other surfer on the island, his mate Allan, were sailing around to these newly discovered waves and surfing them for the first time.

With the long hours of daylight in summer and the sea being warmed by the North Atlantic current, an offshoot of the Gulf Stream, the island's only two surfers seemed to spend almost the whole summer in the waves. During August the holidaymakers arrived, including a few surfers, and Finn and Allan were only too happy to have some fresh company in the line-up. There were no police on the island and nobody ever locked their doors when they went out; it was that kind of place. If the publican had to go out for an hour or two in the evening he would leave the drinkers to fill their own glasses, record them on a chit and pay for them the following evening. Mr. McNeil might cheat the hated taxman but the islanders would never cheat each other.

One would think that two such fortunate surfers would be happy with their lot but the romantic imagination and wanderlust of the Highlander (or, to be more accurate, the "islander") moved them to look further out towards the western horizon. Like Brock Little surfing Waimea but yearning for the bigger stuff on the outer reefs, Finn and Allan could not get Puffin Island out of their minds.

Puffin lay seven miles west of their own island and was so-called because it was inhabited by thousands of puffins in summer as well as seagulls. There had once been a monastery on it in the Middle Ages where the monks could pray in splendid isolation and there was a latter day superstition that it was haunted by the spirit of the last monk to die there who was reputed to have gone mad.

Like a fortress, much of Puffin's foreshore consisted of precipitous, rocky cliffs that rose to heights of a hundred and thirty feet. From what they could see from their own island it looked particularly forbidding but what would the other side be like? With nothing between Puffin Island and Nova Scotia the waves would have plenty of time to grow in power and size and, if like their own island, there were some sandy coves on the western side, then surely it was worth investigating?

Finn prevailed on his father to build them a larger boat that could carry a decent outboard motor and, as autumn turned into winter, they applied themselves to their studies at the island's only school and dreamt of a new island to surf in the summer.

Mr. McNeil worked throughout the winter on the new vessel which they named *Discovery* – not only after Captain Cook's ship but also because discovery of (hopefully) new surfing spots was the purpose for which she was built.

This was their last year at school and, as soon as their exams were over, Finn and Allan began preparations for what they called "Operation Puffin". They took *Discovery* for sea trials around their own island and then, on a sunny morning when the North Atlantic was unusually calm, they took on enough fuel for a voyage of investigation to Puffin and back.

With eager eyes and hopeful hearts they reached their destination shortly after 9 a.m. and began a circumnavigation. On the side of Puffin that faced their own island there was nowhere to land – just one long castle like cliff – but, when they got round to the western side, the calm sea became more turbulent and they saw immense and beautifully formed waves coming in from the west.

There was a small, sandy bay where the waves were breaking off the rocky point and washing up on the beach; it was definitely the best point break that either of them had ever seen but how could they get their boat through the surf which was breaking with such force? They didn't relish being shipwrecked before they had even landed.

They sailed on around the island looking for a place to land but without success. How could the Almighty do this to them? Tempt them with the sight of such a wonderful point break and yet deny them the use of it? Was this some new form of penance that Puffin was inflicting on its visitors – just like the medieval monks who wore coarse horse hair next to their skin so as to give them an itch?

"There must be some way," declared Finn as they sailed around the island for the second time. There was but they didn't find it until after two in the afternoon when the tide began to fall, thereby exposing a great arch of rock where, if they ducked their heads low enough, they could sail through it and into what appeared to be a deep sea cave.

They discussed it for a few minutes and then took the plunge, steering the boat through the dark hole and hoping to find a landing place inside. As they entered the sunless chamber their senses were assailed on all sides – the gloom, the echoes that broke the eerie silence and a powerful smell of sea and kelp.

The sea cave got deeper and sometimes wider and sometimes narrower. It was like being in another world. About two hundred yards in they came to a small, sandy beach which seemed to be illuminated from above. Allan turned off the motor and they put down the anchor in two feet of water. They then got out to explore their landing place.

Rising up from the small stretch of sand were steep, sloping cliffs that opened up to the sky above – like the shaft of a mine. They climbed about eighty feet to the sunlit surface and then sat down to view their discovery.

From their vantage point on the flat top of Puffin they were able to see their own island seven miles to the east, its volcanic cone dominating the horizon like a sentinel. In the background across the seascape they could see other mountainous islands rising out of the vast ocean – sublime, remote and magnificent. It was like sitting on a stage and looking out at creation. Nothing but mountains, islands and sea.

They walked across the springy turf to a break in the cliffs that led down to the cove with the perfect point break. In the bowl of the valley was a sheltered glade with a spring of fresh water from which they quenched their thirst; it was cool, clear and sweet. This, they decided, was where they would build their summer house.

They sat for a while and watched the surf breaking over the point, waves that had been breaking since the beginning of time and which no surfer had ever ridden. At one end of the cove the rocky foreshore became positively Gothic in its architecture; curious as to what lay around the corner, they made their way around basaltic pillars and discovered a new and smaller sea cave where the waves came right in so that they could ride their boards right inside it. Uluwatu without the crowds. Inside the chamber the boom and crash of the waves was like the playing of an orchestra.

They then made their way to the south side of the island where they discovered the ruins of the old monastery and some crumbling gravestones of the monks. They wondered if they were the first people to step on the land since the last monk died towards the end of the Middle Ages. They checked some of the broken down stones with a view to using them for the shelter which, in their imaginations, they were already building down in the glade. Like their Norse seafaring ancestors, they had discovered their treasure and planned to use it to their advantage.

The sun was starting to set over the western sea so, in order to avoid being trapped by the tide, they drove their boat out of the cave and back into the ocean for the voyage home.

The next time they travelled to Puffin Island their boat was laden with surfboards, wetsuits, repair kit, preserved food, a sack of potatoes, fishing lines, tools, shotguns and ammunition and even some live hens to lay fresh eggs. They timed their trip to reach the entrance to the sea cave at the lowest point of the tide. Then, after unloading all their gear and carting it up the hill and down into the glade, they donned wetsuits, picked up their boards and ran into the sea to surf the new spot which they called Perfection Point.

For Finn it lived up to its name on his first wave which was fast, long and beautifully formed as it rolled over the reef that protruded from the point. It was far better than anything they had ever ridden on their own island and was followed by more of the same. So many wonderful waves and only two guys to ride them. As they lay on their boards waiting for the next set Allan called out some lines from *The Ancient Mariner*:

"The air breeze blew, the white foam flew,
The furrow followed free;
We were the first that ever burst
Into that silent sea."

Back on land they started the work of carrying the loose grey stones from the ruined monastery to the new building site where, using the dry stone wall approach, they constructed a small shack for shelter and sleeping. It had a waterproof roof of thatch, a chimney and a door that opened. Like Adam and Eve in the Garden of Eden, they were creating a whole new world from scratch.

For food they prised mussels and other shellfish off the rocks and caught sea trout and grey mullet with their fishing lines. They shot puffins and other birds which they put in the pot of soup that they boiled over the camp fire. And, like their ancestors, they added edible seaweed like dulse and carragheen to the soup.

Throughout the summer they would stay on the island for a few days and nights at a time and then return home for more provisions and a bit of contact with the rest of the human race.

As time went on they shared their secret with a few other surfers whom they would ferry out to Puffin Island for days of waves and nights of sitting around the camp fire feasting, laughing and drinking just like the Vikings used to do when they came over to Britain on their missions of rape and pillage.

As with every happy band of handsome surfers, Puffin Island soon became a magnet for the girls. Finn chose only the best looking ones so that they could fit in with the natural beauty of the island. And, since he was the one with the boat, he had the final say. Tents sprouted around the stone walled structure and great fun was had by all as they enjoyed nature in its purest form.

In choosing whom to invite to the island to share the wave on Perfection Point Finn took into account musical talents; he felt that, although a stereo powered by a car battery could provide no end of sound and volume, something more suited to the natural sounds of the island – the wind, the waves and the birds – could only enhance the quality of their *après-surf* activities. Thus it was that those surfers who could play guitar, mouth organ or drums found that they were particularly welcome. Finn knew how closely surfing and music are linked, with both relying on rhythm, energy and imagination. Cut off from the rest of the world, they made their own music and their own fun from the island's resources and their own creativity.

On some nights, when they got really out of it, their twisted minds believed that they saw the mad monk. Finn saw him first and told the others that he had six fingers on each hand and six toes on each foot and that he hovered about two feet above the ground, his black monk's cowl blowing in the breeze.

Finn believed that the monk, being a lover of solitude, resented their intrusion but Allan retorted that the strange sounds they heard at night were nothing more than the island adjusting to human beings after a gap of approximately six centuries. But Finn wasn't convinced.

He didn't want to bring a priest out to conduct an exorcism as he feared that, once he saw how you could land in the sea cave, he might reclaim the island for the Church and kick them all off.

Instead, they decided to have a Viking party where they would all dress up as Vikings and, with their spears, prowl around the island at night in one mass act of exorcism.

They chose Midsummer Night for this all important ritual which, in reality, was only an excuse to have a wild party. They felt that a night of excessive hedonism would not only exorcise the ghost of the mad monk but also bring some much needed balance to the island after all the self-flagellation and other acts of debasement before God of its previous monastic inhabitants. It was now time for the island to have some fun.

After finishing their late afternoon surf at Perfection Point the surfing crew and their girl-friends spent several hours making costumes out of pieces of material and large leaves and their spears out of tree branches. Most of the guys already had long, blond hair and so there was no need for the wigs that are normally in such demand for a Viking costume party.

With the uniforms and spears and the wine and the weed came a reversion to a rather primitive state and, for the first time in twelve hundred years, the island resounded to the screams and war-cries of wild Vikings who rampaged around it like men and women possessed, poking their sharp spears madly at anything that moved. It was all too much for the six-fingered monk; his ghost was never seen again. As Finn said afterwards, "exorcist" is a new word that they could all put on their C.V.s.

Around 4 a.m. the first rays of light began to appear on the eastern horizon and it was time to swap Viking clothes for wetsuits and wooden spears for sticks of fibreglass.

Finn was the first one in the water and, in the improving light, he paddled out to where the waves were breaking so cleanly over the reef.

As he stood up on his board and steered it across the face of the breaking wave he felt ever so powerful. The wave was his, the new day was his and the island was his. At seventeen he was king of his own universe and he even had the power to exorcise demons and ghosts. "Thanks, Huey," he cried as the wave broke and gave him a magic ride.

THE TORQUAY TERRORS

They called themselves the Torquay Terrors but that was not an entirely accurate description. They could be terrors if you were a city dude from Melbourne who came down to their local break at Bells Beach and dropped in on a wave to which they had priority, and some of them looked pretty fearsome with their long, straggly hair, a few tattoos, occasional stubble on their chins and powerful motor bikes that they liked to ride up and down the main street of the small town late at night when there was no traffic and no cops to spoil the fun.

However, beneath all the bravado they wouldn't harm a flea and their attitude to sharing their exceptional surf break with others was eminently reasonable. Although clannishly "local", they made friends with some of the out-of-town surfers who came to Bells and they always entered into the fun of the pro tour that took place there every Easter. Over the years they had got to know – and like – some of the top pros and, of course, for the pros it was always useful to have a local and trusted "contact".

As hard core, all-year-round surfers they did find the week of the pro tour a bit like when the circus comes to town but the spunky, bikini clad beauties that it attracted to the area more than made up for the inconvenience of crowded waves. And, of course, the after-contest party was always a good excuse to get totally wasted.

Although they could handle the contest what they could not deal with were the financial problems of the body that organised it. It was the year 2020 and, after long years of boom, there was now a serious economic recession throughout the Western world. When profits start falling the first thing that companies ditch is doling out wads of money in the form of "sponsorship". And who can blame them?

Golf and tennis were reasonably safe as the leaders of the really big, multi-national companies were in many cases golfers and tennis players themselves whereas it was rare to find a dedicated surfer as a "captain of industry". And so surfing was a long way down the list of sports to be sponsored. And it didn't help that Bruce Baxter, the chief executive of Universal Surfing, the body that organised the pro tour, was as unimpressive in the board room as a captain of industry would be in the waves. Hell, the guy didn't even know how to dress properly when he made his approaches to companies on behalf of surfing – a crumpled purple shirt, gaudy tie and brown leather jacket which made most businessmen cringe and was enough to dissuade them from investing in a sport with such an unprofessional public face.

Things were now so bad for the pro tour that the kitty was as bare as Mother Hubbard's cupboard and the bank was refusing to advance any more funds. This meant that pro surfers – and, even worse, administrators and judges – would not be able to be paid after the end of the current month and the whole pro tour would come to an abrupt halt and would sink forever into the bottomless abyss of Davy Jones' locker. Worst of all Bruce Baxter would be out of a job and, having presided over the demise of world surfing, would hardly be an attractive proposition to any other employer. Something had to be done. In double quick time.

Although the corporate doors seemed to be closed in Australia, America and Europe there was a small beam of hope on the horizon in Japan where the Kikimoko Corporation, the largest producer of high quality sunglasses on the planet, was keen to associate its name with a glamorous sport that was anchored in the sunshine of an eternal summer for which people needed to buy expensive sunglasses.

Bruce Baxter had been in close communication with Mr. Kikimoko and the figure of twelve million dollars had been agreed subject to a few minor conditions, one of which was that Mr. Kikimoko wanted to come to a surf contest to see what exactly it was that his company would be sponsoring. "I must make sure that it is the right image to project to Japanese youth as we don't want them to be led astray by Western decadence, do we?" he had said over the phone from Tokyo.

"What do you mean?" asked a nervous Baxter.

"Things like men with long hair and tattoos. In Japan we associate long hair with rebelliousness and tattoos with organised crime groups like the Yakuza. We want to create a very clean image." So that was it; twelve million dollars and the saving of pro surfing for Mr. Kikimoko's idea of a clean image. In other words his narrow, little slit eyes must be protected from types like the Torquay Terrors.

And, of course, from some of the pro surfers who also had long hair and a couple of whom had tattoos; one had a surfboard etched on his left arm with the leg-rope winding down over the back of his hand and finishing between two of his fingers while the other had a big heart on his upper arm with "I love Susie" written inside it. Only problem was that, shortly after he had it done, Susie, his girl-friend of three years, had run off with the World Champion and, instead of loving Susie he now hated her.

However, the pro surfers were the least of Baxter's worries; they were mere employees of Universal Surfing and would have to do whatever their boss told them. He called a meeting of the contestants who all agreed that it was in their mutual interests to exchange their flowing locks for a more acceptable "short back and sides" for the Bell's Beach contest while the surfer with the tattooed surfboard on his arm would wear a wetsuit to cover it up and Susie's boyfriend decided that now was the time to get the tattoo with such painful memories removed once and for all.

That dealt with the surfers but what about the spectators? After all, for a sponsoring company seeking mass sales they are the most important ingredient of all. Baxter could hardly run a contest without spectators but would all the spectators meet with Mr. Kikimoko's approval? Types like the Torquay Terrors. They would have to be kept off the beach and out of sight.

With the small amount of funds that were left in Universal Surfing's coffers Baxter paid a Melbourne security firm to send down its army of goons not just to patrol the contestants' enclosure on the stand but the whole beach.

Entry to the beach would be by ticket and tickets would be handed out only to clean shaven chaps with neat haircuts and no tattoos. A bit like a swanky nightclub which has a guard on the door to say who may

204

and may not enter the establishment. And, in order to pack as many people of the right sort on to the beach to impress Mr. Kikimoko, Baxter set up a couple of bikini clad girl hairdressers to give free haircuts and, to put the icing on the cake, a free head massage as well.

This drew a few customers – mostly those who were about to make an appointment for a haircut anyway and decided that a free one by a girl whose all but naked breasts would rub against the head during cutting and whose slender fingers would massage the head at the end of it was as good a deal as any. But the Torquay Terrors would have none of it.

Although Baxter knew that the goons would keep them and their type off the beach he was still worried that they might roar around the streets on their motor bikes or otherwise bring themselves to the attention of Mr. Kikimoko.

"Listen, you guys," said Baxter on the day before the contest. "You run the risk of giving surfing a bad name."

"Why?" asked an amazed Eddie.

"We've got Mr. Kikimoko arriving to-morrow. He's going to be the saviour of pro surfing. In fact, he's prepared to rescue the tour by putting twelve million dollars into the sport of surfing."

"Well bully for him!" exclaimed Dan.

"Yes, but he won't if he sees people like you."

"Why, what's wrong with us?"

"Well, it's just an image problem. I'm sure here's nothing wrong with you but Mr. Kikimoko loesn't like long hair or tattoos or things like that. Why lon't you go off on a surfing trip for a few days? There

205

are some great beaches further along the coast where the waves won't be crowded with contest surfers."

"Are you trying to tell us that we are no longer welcome in our own town?"

"Well, not really. But surely you can oblige for just a few days. He'll be on the plane back to Japan on Tuesday and then you can come back. I don't think that's much to ask for twelve million dollars of sponsorship money."

"Now let's get this right," said Andy. "You are ordering us to leave the town where we live so that we won't expose our ugly faces to some rich Jap who is about to put twelve million dollars into Universal Surfing which will be used exclusively for the benefit of forty-four surfers and a few administrators like yourself?"

"You don't have to leave. As long as you keep a low profile. We don't want to give the wrong impression."

"We'll see," they said as they walked away from the bizarre conversation.

Of course, the Terrors were not the only ones who might not pass muster with the sensitive Mr Kikimoko and so Baxter, worried that some wretched surfers might sink the whole deal by their appearance, went to the local police commander, explained his problem and asked if the cops could arrest "undesirables" and hold them in the cells for a few days until the end of the contest.

"Unfortunately, Mr. Baxter, as much as I would like to accede to your eminently sensible request I am unable to do so. Some wretched thing called habeas corpus which has its roots in Magna Carta. It prevents us

206

from arresting and detaining people unless we produce them in court on a charge. And, since having long hair or tattoos or not shaving for a couple of days are not yet against the law, we can not arrest them."

"Can't you plant some drugs on them?" asked an increasingly desperate Baxter. "If you do that, I'll use a few thousand out of the twelve million to make a donation to the police refreshment fund."

"We just don't have the manpower. It's Easter week-end and we have been ordered by headquarters to target motorists and shower them with speeding tickets and to leave everything else alone. We have got a speeding ticket target to meet and it is a lot higher than twelve million. I'm sorry but the police can't help you – much as I would like to. I've always hated this habeas corpus nonsense; the police would be a lot happier if we could detain indefinitely those whom we think should be locked up but sadly we're stuck with habeas corpus. It's part of the rights of the people and unfortunately they won't part with it."

When Kikimoko arrived at Melbourne Airport on the first morning of the contest he was driven by Baxter through the outer suburbs of Melbourne and then across green fields to the coastal settlement of Torquay. "Ah, so much space," said Mr. Kikimoko. "I like it very much. Clean, green image – very good."

He was happy with his hotel and on the official stand everybody put him on a great fuss, knowing that the future of pro surfing depended on his impending sponsorship.

The sun shone all day, the waves were big and gnarly and the surfing was awesome. And all the spectators looked nice. Mr. Kikimoko seemed to be happy with all that he saw but he did stress to Baxter that he wanted to see all sides of the contest before finally making up his mind on the sponsorship deal.

Baxter was sweating. Deep down he knew that Mr. Kikimoko's expectations were the complete antithesis of the reality of a surf contest and of surfing in general. The challenge was to keep up the façade until the last day when the deal was due to be signed and Mr. Kikimoko would be on the plane back to Tokyo. Then Universal Surfing would have its money and surfing at Torquay could get back to normal.

"Why should we put up with a jumped-up punk like Baxter speaking to us like that?" asked Eddie. "I reckon we've been jolly reasonable over the years welcoming the pros here for a week when they take over the waves and the town and then leave to go off somewhere else. Locals should at least be respected and not be spoken to like that. Nor should they be kept off the beach by an army of fat goons from the city."

"I agree," said Ron, "especially since the money will go only to a precious few and that does not include us or anyone else in Torquay."

"So we do something about it?"

"Why not?"

"Let's start from basics. Anything we do to assert the rights of true surfers – people like us – can only be good for surfing in general. If the price of having a pro tour is to cleanse the beach of real surfers, then it's a price not worth paying. Even if we manage to sink the deal, it wouldn't be the end of the world. People would still surf. Some other form of pro surfing would emerge out of the ruins – uncontaminated by the likes of Baxter and his Jap friend."

208

They spread the story among their fellow locals, every one of whom was outraged to think that they were regarded as nothing more than a bit of effluent to be air-brushed off their own beach to meet the temporary financial needs of a creep like Baxter.

After several local surfers had been refused entry by the goons a "Reclaim the Beach" movement began and grew like a mushroom after a shower of rain. It was not confined to the locals as there was seething anger among those who had come from afar and had been refused entry to the beach because of their appearance. In the pub that night certain plans were made.

It was to be a two pronged attack – by land and sea. More than a hundred surfers would paddle out from the next beach and then move on to the contest wave and ride it for as long as they liked. This "reclaiming of the waves" would put an end to the heats as how could a contestant get any points with a hundred others out there? And, of course, the hundred other surfers had all been refused entry to the beach; in other words, their appearance was not to Mr. Kikimoko's liking.

While all this was taking place in the waves there would be a simultaneous pincer movement from behind the stands from about five hundred disaffected surfers, bikies, rugby players, local hoons and others who, by sheer weight of numbers, would barge their way on to the beach and then do whatever they liked. "Reclaim the beach" was their cry even though, in the case of the bikies and the rugby players, they hadn't been on the beach in years.

Like a military invasion the two attacks were timed to coincide so as to produce the maximum mayhem in one decisive swoop.

To get through the security barrier that surrounded the beach the army of five hundred decided to target individual goons and overpower them one by one.

Most of the goons so targeted simply gave up as they were guards and not fighting soldiers but one fool decided to resist. No problem. They simply belted him in his fat stomach and down he went.

The way was now open and they poured through the gap on to the beach, took over the sound system, blared out some heavy metal, let off fireworks and started a great big party.

Most of the spectators joined in the screaming, singing and dancing as the heats in the water had been fairly boring and this was at least different. They had come only for a surf contest and were now getting a party thrown in as well.

And those in the contestants' enclosure on the stands? They just glared down at all these brazen anarchists and refused to leave their seats and join in the party on the sand. Until, that is, someone rang up the contest organiser on a mobile phone and made a bomb scare and so the stands had to be emptied.

There was no bomb but nobody wanted to return to the stands as both administrators and contestants believed that these people were so mad that letting off bombs was probably part of their everyday behaviour.

Baxter tried to shield Mr. Kikimoko's eyes from the awful sight of his contest descending into chaos but it was too late. Mr. Kikimoko decided that, if Universal

Surfing couldn't even organise a contest to proceed in an orderly manner, how on earth could they be trusted with his sponsorship money? This sort of disorder was not the type of thing that his squeaky clean and ever so profitable company wanted to be associated with.

The Bells Beach contest of 2020 did not even produce a winner but it went down in surfing history, together with that crazy contest at Huntington Beach when they set fire to the stands, as the most memorable.

Mr. Kikimoko flew back to Japan without writing a sponsorship cheque. Baxter jumped off a rocky point and his body was washed up on Bells Beach. The pro tour could go no further and, as predicted, sank into the ocean. But only for a time.

As the Terrors predicted, out of the ashes rose a new, smaller and better organisation that arranged contests that were much closer to the true spirit of surfing. There was less money, more fun and better waveriding.

The new circuit was started and funded by a group of small surf companies in and around Torquay which, after all, was where Australia's surfing culture began. The fact was that the pro tour had gone too far too fast and needed to get back to the roots of surfing. In the wider scheme of things the Torquay Terrors, with their long hair and tattoos, had proved themselves far more valuable to surfing than even the most generous sponsor.

WRONG WAY, RIGHT WAY

Rory was one of a group that called themselves the "Urban Surfers". They lived in the suburb of Midland which is about as far away from Perth's beaches as it is possible to go without actually being in the countryside and so every trip to the waves was a bit of a mission. But the rewards always made it worthwhile.

Since they were so few in numbers in this non-surfing suburb the Urban Surfers were a close knit band who seemed to have as much fun out of the waves as in them. Young, carefree and reckless, these party loving beasts lived for the moment and took whatever it gave them without fear of the consequences.

On this particular Saturday they had surfed for several hours in head high waves at Cottesloe Beach, played a bit of beach cricket with the locals and then gone back to Midland to celebrate Rory's eighteenth birthday.

The boy himself over-indulged in everything that was going and the others were not too far behind. When the first light of dawn started to peep through the windows Rory looked around the party room at the mess – empty beer cans and wine bottles, roaches and overflowing ashtrays, an empty tube of lipstick, a pair of girl's lace knickers hanging on the pot plant and several people crashed out on the couches and floor. It looked like the aftermath of a tank battle.

However, unlike the others, Rory was still standing and a new day was dawning - the first day of his nineteenth year. He looked at his watch. It was ten past six which, he reflected, was exactly the time that he had arrived in this mad world eighteen years ago. Suddenly he felt a surge of energy, confidence and superiority as he looked at his comatose mates, branding them as "pikers" who were unable to last the distance. "I'm going for an early morning surf," he decided. "I'll hitch a ride down to the beach."

Rory was not so far "out of it" as to be unaware of his less than sober state and so he took great care in preparing for his early morning mission to the waves. He was wearing jeans and a t-shirt but remembered to put on a warm jersey as the early morning air could be quite nippy. Into a bag he packed his wetsuit as well as some wax and he then tucked a fifty dollar note in his pocket to buy some breakfast and lunch as well as his newly acquired credit card.

His board was still in its bag from the day before. He put its strap over his shoulder and, remembering to pick up the bag, he gently opened the front door. A couple of minutes later he was walking down the quiet street to the main highway which brought the traffic into Perth from the east and then ran down through the city to the Indian Ocean. To the waves.

By the time he reached the highway the effects of his night of excess were beginning to tell and the poor boy was starting to feel tired and confused.

In order to hitch to the beach he needed to cross the highway but such an exercise was now beyond both his legs and his mind. Instead he just sat down on the near side of the highway and lethargically put out his thumb.

A few minutes later he heard a car stop. He opened his eyes and had the vague impression of an

213

MGBGT in the colours of British Racing Green reversing towards him.

It pulled to a stop a few feet away and the driver, a friendly young chap in his early thirties, got out and asked Rory where he wanted to go. "To the waves," he replied.

"They're rather a long way," said the driver.

"They always are. That's the problem with living in Midland."

"So, do you want a ride?"

"Of course."

By now the driver had produced straps to tie the surfboard on to the roof racks of the small sports car and Rory managed to lift the board up for them to secure it. He then climbed into the passenger seat and promptly fell asleep.

"Oh well," thought the driver, "if he sleeps now, he'll be able to talk to me later on when it will be more important to stay awake." And off they went.

Five hours later Rory woke up as the car came to a fairly sudden stop at a petrol station. He wiped his eyes and asked, "Where are we?"

"In the middle of the Nullabor Plain."

"But I'm meant to be at Cottesloe Beach. How did I get here?"

"I guess you hitch hiked on the wrong side of the road."

"Ahhhhh!"

"So, you can either get out of the car and hitch your way back – on the right side of the road – or you can stay in the car."

"Where are you going?"

"To the Gold Coast. That's where I live. We should be there by Tuesday morning; that's when I have to be back at work." Rory went to wind down the window. "Don't do that," said the driver.

"Why?"

"Because of the rats. I don't want the smell to get into the car."

"Rats?"

"Yes, there's a plague of them. The drought in the Great Victorian Desert has driven them down here where there's still a bit of vegetation for them to feed on. I saw them when I drove across to Perth on Thursday."

"Thursday! You drove all the way from the Gold Coast to Perth for only two days?"

"Yes. I do it every second week-end. My girl friend lives in Perth and so we spend the whole time together in bed. Every other week-end I go surfing on the Gold Coast."

"So what do you do?"

"I'm an orthodontist in Surfers' Paradise."

By now the rats were running over the bonnet of the car. Rory wiped his eyes again and looked outside. The flat ground was carpeted with brown rats as far as the eye could see. They were literally "shoulder to shoulder" as they moved this way and that – like a wave. They were running up and down the petrol pumps and the poles while the petrol station manager, a moronic looking fellow with an exceptionally big head, had his long trousers tucked into his socks to stop them running up the insides of his legs.

Trampling on top of them the big headed one made his way over to the driver's window. "Fill her up," said the driver who by now had introduced himself to Rory as "Carl".

When the tank was filled the guy came up to the window and Carl squeezed a fifty dollar note and a twenty through the glass and told him to keep the change. It was better than having to get out of the car and step over the rats.

Even though the window was pulled down only a couple of inches the rat smell came powering into the car and Rory started to feel sick. "How on earth do you put up with the rats?" he asked the big headed one.

"You just get used to them," he drawled. He then went inside the petrol station, stood on top of the counter and started dancing with his wife, whose head was just as big as his.

"They're all inbred in these parts," explained Carl, "and the isolation – no neighbours for a hundred miles either side – sends them bonkers. Now what do you want to do? Get out here and hitch hike or carry on?"

"I'll carry on," said Rory who was beginning to wonder if he was still on Planet Earth.

Off they went, the tyres of the sports car squashing and killing the rats as they drove. It was another sixty miles before the rats began to thin out and eventually they disappeared altogether.

"How will they ever get rid of them?" asked a bewildered Rory.

"When they run out of vegetation they start eating each other," explained Carl. "That's what happened the last time they moved down here from the desert about five years ago."

It was night time when they crossed the border into South Australia and they stopped at a roadhouse for supper.

Just after Carl announced that they would have to pull into a lay-by for a few hours' kip Rory put his hand in his pocket to get some money to pay for his meal – and for Carl's – when he found some tabs of speed that were left over from the party. He gave one to Carl and so they were able to keep driving for another few hours.

They finally went to sleep about 4 a.m. and woke up at eight for Day Two of their trans-Australia expedition.

They drove through the barren countryside and the only signs of life were the occasional passing motorist (mostly trucks) and one or two inland towns with names like Broken Hill and Wilcannia.

In the afternoon the countryside became greener and flocks of sheep could be seen here and there as the MGBGT made its way through western New South Wales.

With the help of another of Rory's little pills Carl drove through most of Monday night as well, stopping only for three hours' sleep.

The golden sun was rising over the blue Pacific as the faithful sports car came over the hill on the way from Lismore down to the coast. Rory, by now fully alert and impressionable after spending many hours asleep in the passenger's seat, was entranced by all that he saw – vegetation far greener and more lush than anything he had ever seen in Western Australia, pineapple plantations, sugar cane fields and the magnificent east coast in the freshness of a new day. And signposts to famous surf breaks that he had read

217

about in the mags – places like Lennox Head, Byron Bay and Kirra.

The hairs started to tingle on his head as he thought of the excitement of having his first surf in the Pacific Ocean; for the occasion the waves were big and were breaking ever so cleanly all the way up the coast.

The thrill of being back in his natural habitat also affected Carl as he described the different breaks with enthusiasm and personal anecdotes.

"I would appreciate if you could drop me off at Burleigh Heads," said Rory as Carl started to explain the best way to ride the famous wave.

"This is going to be the greatest day of my life," said a beaming Rory.

"Better than Cottesloe?" asked Carl.

"Yes, of course. And all because I was so stupid that I hitch hiked on the wrong side of the road."

"Maybe you shouldn't get so 'out of it' at parties," said Carl.

Rory watched another perfect wave breaking over the point. "Or maybe I should."

PENCARROW POINT

Riding the excellent wave at Pencarrow Point was very much a local affair. A long way off the beaten track in a remote part of Cornwall, it was a bit of a secret spot that the local surfers cherished and treated as their own special playground. Well, not quite their own.

On the other side of the point was a marine base and on some days the marines would do their boat drill — both rowing boats and outboard motors. This never really bothered the surfers as, for obvious reasons, the marines chose days when the waves were small enough for them to get their boats through to the beach without mishap and these were generally days when the surfers were not out. Thus there was a good relationship between these two very different users of the sea. Until, that is, the government closed down the base in yet another penny-pinching "defence cut". And so the marines moved out of their sixty acre coastal base and it was mothballed.

"I guess the waves are better now that we have them entirely to ourselves," said seventeen year old Greg Sutton one night at the family dinner table.

"Maybe," replied his father, "but I'd be much happier if they were still there."

"Why?"

"It's never good to see such a valuable property lying idle. Not from the economic point of view but you never know what the government will do with it. These days governments never seem to do the right thing and I fear that an empty base is an accident waiting to happen."

"Don't be so pessimistic," said his wife. "I'm sure it won't be put to a wrong use."

"We'll see,"

A few months after this conversation the mothballed base appeared to be coming to life. Lorries and workmen were coming and going but nobody knew for what purpose. And most of the work seemed to be done in the dead of night when the locals were all in bed.

The surfers were naturally curious because of the proximity of the old base to the surf break where they spent so many hours of their lives. Some said that it was going to be a new boarding school, some opted for a housing development while others said that it was going to be the setting for a new movie.

Then the new inhabitants started to arrive – late at night and in luxury coaches with blackened windows and police escorts. The old marine base was now a centre for asylum seekers – all two and a half thousand of them – and not a word had been breathed by the authorities to any of the locals. It was all done surreptitiously – just like when the government uses holiday periods like Easter and Christmas, when many people are away, to slip through some of the nastier laws that take away people's rights. And so the lovely, friendly and remote surfing spot – and indeed their whole way of life – was to be changed forever by distant and faceless forces in London that were beyond their control.

After the first three days of these thousands of foreign invaders roaming around the place the houses of Pencarrow had more burglaries than in the past ten years. "We may as well be living in the Congo or Afghanistan," declared an angry Mr. Sutton.

Young men from Africa and the Middle East started to harass the local girls and pick fights with the boys. And, if anyone complained to the police about the upheaval to their nice little town and the crime wave it was producing, they were accused of being "racists" and were threatened with prosecution under the Race Relations Act.

Greg and his friends spent more time than ever in the ocean. Not only was Pencarrow Point getting a decent swell but the sea was one of the few places one could go to get away from all these unwanted intruders. Until, that is, the government provided them with sports equipment that included a hundred brand new surfboards and hundreds of wetsuits in different sizes.

This angered Greg and all the other surfers who had had to save up to buy their own surfboards and wetties and didn't see why asylum seekers on the make should be provided with free ones by the taxpayer.

As soon as they got hold of the surfboards a hundred young men from Iraq, West Africa and other such places took over the ocean, dropping in on waves that they couldn't even ride and generally acting like hoons.

When Greg and the others tried to explain to them that you don't drop in on a wave to which another surfer had prior claim, it was like talking to a brick wall. The asylum seekers claimed that they couldn't understand English yet they kept screaming, "Do not speak to us like that. We have our human rights."

The asylum seekers had all day to surf on their expensive boards while the others had to go to school and work. Naturally the boys looked forward to the dusk session in the waves but it was no longer a pleasure as they were dropped in on virtually every time.

They were faced with the choice of either giving up surfing or standing up for their rights and, like all true surfers, they chose the latter. Nobody had ever thrown a punch in the waves at Pencarrow Point but the crew decided that, everything else having failed, physical force was now the only viable option.

"Okay," screamed Greg. "The next time one of you bludgers drops in on a local, that's it. You can't say I didn't warn you." Whether they understood it or not he didn't know but on the very next wave a young Arab with a moustache dropped in on Max who, like Greg, had lived at Pencarrow Point all his life. Max kept going and collided with the guy. Wipeout. They waited until the chap retrieved his board and paddled back to where the waves were breaking.

He was then assailed by half a dozen of the local crew who gave him a thorough beating. A couple of other asylum seekers paddled over and they too were punched as all of them had been dropping in all the afternoon – in fact, ever since they made their unwelcome appearance in the sea on their fancy new surfboards.

One by one the locals cleared the waves of the uninvited guests with the result that they had their best surf in weeks. It was just like old times again and they hoped that the word would spread around the camp that the waves were no longer safe for asylum seekers who didn't know how to surf. All they wanted was to be left alone.

However, a crowd of Africans and Arabs was assembling on the beach and they looked threatening – shaking their fists in the air and screaming "We have our human rights".

So as to avoid any further confrontation the boys stayed out in the waves until dark and then paddled much further down the beach so as to come in at a point near their homes. They were now afraid to go out on their own at night in their own town. But they weren't allowed to complain or say anything as that would be "racist".

However, it soon became obvious that their real enemy was not the asylum seekers but the mischief making "human rights" lawyers who stood behind them on every matter and stirred up as much trouble as they could between the asylum seekers and the locals because the more trouble meant more legal fees in the pockets of the lawyers.

The next day in the camp these "human rights" lawyers went around taking statements from all those who had been in the water during the confrontation and then, armed with these, called the police and laid all sorts of charges against the local surfers.

Greg and his friends were arrested and charged with assault. As they entered the courthouse they were photographed by the tabloids. Later they saw their photos plastered across the front page under the headline "Racists who beat up poor asylum seekers in the sea".

Of course, they were all convicted and sent to prison as the magistrate was too scared to do anything else. If he had let them off with only a fine he too would have been vilified in the papers as a "racist".

When they came out of jail they tried to get back into surfing as the best way to get their lives back on track but the problem was worse than ever. While they had been "inside" the ever generous government had provided more surfboards as one of the social workers had "sent it up the line" that surfing was a good way for the poor asylum seekers to fill in their long and idle days. The result was that there were no longer any waves to ride, such were the crowds of alien, wave wrecking novices.

More trouble between the two groups broke out in a pub one night when some of the asylum seekers started hassling the blonde barmaid. The fighting got so bad that the police arrived in flak jackets – as in a battle situation – to try to restore order.

Pencarrow Point was now a war zone but, when the editor of the local newspaper wrote an accurate report of what had happened at the pub, the police threatened to arrest him for "inciting racial hatred".

Since there was no longer much point in living in their once peaceful little town any longer the boys decided to consult the town's lawyer, an old chap called Harry Benson, to see if there was anything they could do to get back some of the rights and pleasures that had been taken from them.

"I'm afraid I can't help you," he said. "Under the new Human Rights Act these people have all the rights in the world but at the expense of the traditional and very real rights of the British people. Welcome to the new Britain. It's not a place that I feel comfortable in although I thought that down here in this distant neck of the woods we could hold on to the old ways a bit longer than elsewhere. But I was wrong."

"So what can we do?"

"If I was your age I'd emigrate."

"But we've grown up together!"

"Then emigrate together."

And that is exactly what they did. They scraped together what money they could and went on a long surfing safari in warm climates. It ended in sunny Queensland where they took jobs and settled down and became citizens of a country that they felt more at home in than where they had grown up. None of them ever went back to England. None of them wanted to. England's loss was Australia's gain.

TO PARIS FOR THE DAY

Despite having some of the best waves in the world breaking on its Atlantic coast France has never produced a world class surfer. An important reason for this is that, if one gets into the Top 10 in France, one is given so much sponsorship, free boards and clothes, glowing publicity in magazines and endless trips to nice surfing spots in warm weather that there is not really any incentive to lift one's performance. Just hang in there in the Top 10 and enjoy a very comfortable existence.

For years tens of thousands of French people have gathered on the beach at Biarritz and Hossegor and Lacanau to cheer Australian and American champions who take all the prizes, make their winning speeches in English and then fly out of France the next day, their pockets overflowing with the prize money put up by French companies. Those wretched Anglo-Saxons!

Which was why Olivier was such a freak. Known as 'the flying Basque" because of his aerials, this Biarrot (native of Biarritz) had surged on to the world surfing scene like an out-of-control meteorite and was sweeping all before him. He set his sights higher than just staying in the Top 10 in France. The World Championship was what he wanted and nothing less.

Olivier's awesome surfing ability was complemented by his film star looks, natural charm, perfect manners and considerable intellectual ability. It seemed that God had put him on earth to be an exceptional surfer and to lift France out of her current doldrums as the Fifth Republic was creaking at the

226

foundations and in some ways resembled the *ancien regime* before 1789. It no longer seemed to work and the people's attention had to be directed towards things like national sports successes, new movies, the lives of celebrities and a carefully crafted anti-Americanism.

By some freak of organisation – dictated by sponsorship considerations – the pro tour for this year had been crammed into the first eight months and, instead of finishing in the big waves of Hawaii, was culminating in the smaller waves of south-west France.

The last contest was at Hossegor and Olivier went into it in first equal place with Jared Barker of California. Oh, the tension! This was far more than a surfing contest as the French were now in such a state of chaos and decline that the only thing that made them feel good was to get one over the Americans. This was not Olivier v. Jared but France v. America. If Olivier could pull it off it would be the greatest French success since they won the soccer World Cup. So much was riding on it that both the President and the Prime Minister had flown down from Paris to watch the action in the waves.

All this hype might have put off a lesser surfer but Olivier remained splendidly unfazed and got down to doing what he did best – riding waves and putting the points on the board.

As if God Himself had taken an interest in the matter both surfers got through to the Final from opposite ends of the draw. So here they were on the beach break between Les Estagnots and Hossegor main beach in glorious sunshine, perfect eight foot waves and an excited crowd on the beach of seventy thousand people.

A roar of encouragement accompanied Olivier as he ran down the beach in his boardshorts and into the waves for his neck and neck heat with Jared. Each of them selected their waves with care and rode them with effortless superiority. Jared got a tube on his first wave and Olivier matched it with one of his trademark aerials.

On the next one the Frenchman executed a first class floater which earned him a good score but Jared got another barrel. It was more like an expression session than a contest heat and the crowd was loving every minute of it.

It seemed that Jared was slightly ahead but then just before the hooter sounded, Olivier got the most magical barrel that he rode to perfection. He got a ten And the finalist's prize. And the World Championship Oh, the delirium on the beach!

Ten thousand almost naked girls ran into the sea to touch him and the only way Olivier could get back to the beach was to tie himself into the harness that was lowered to him by a hovering helicopter overhead. Thus did he leapfrog over the mass of soft, tanned flesh, his feet swinging only a few inches above the squealing groupies. One of them, who was wearing only a tiny g-string, managed to jump so high that she grabbed the harness and flew with Olivier to the winner's stand, giving him a full massage en route.

On the winner's stand the new champion was drenched by a rainfall of champagne and was greeted with a Number One handshake by the President of France who had been drinking champagne in the sun all the afternoon and, insecure as ever, was deliriously happy that Olivier had put one over the Americans.

The President was invited to the microphone first and to the hushed crowd he confided his delight and declared Olivier the "Saviour of French honour". Then, with his head still swimming in champers and his brain a little addled, he said, "Because this champion has France in his hands he may make any wish and it will be granted." With that he flopped down in his chair and had another drink.

All eyes were now on Olivier who was squatting down on his haunches writing things in a notebook. The champagne was still dripping out of his brown, curly hair. He kept on writing for nearly four minutes. Everyone thought he was being very funny by writing out such a long wish list.

Eventually he stood up and walked to the microphone, he and Jared being the only sober ones in the official enclosure. At last the French were going to hear a winner's speech in their own beautiful language.

"Mr. President, ladies and gentlemen and fellow surfers," he said in French. "This is a magic moment for me. It is a great thrill to be World Champion but it was an even bigger thrill to be inside that last barrel." Cheers from the surfers and a look of bewilderment on the faces of the President, the Prime Minister and all the other non-surfers. "I am very grateful for the support of my home crowd." Squeals of delight from the ten thousand naked girls. "I wish to thank my opponent, Jared from California, who is also my good friend, for his contribution to the contest. Thanks also to the sponsor, the organisers and everyone else who has made this into the perfect contest."

He then looked up at the sun and blew a kiss to it. Then one to the waves. He went to sit down. Then, with a contrived gesture as if he had forgotten something important, he returned to the microphone and looked at the smiling President. "You very graciously promised to grant me a wish, Sir." he said.

"Yes," said the President. "Are you thinking of the Legion of Honour?"

"No, I am not old enough to wear decorations around my neck. I have one wish. It is short and simple and one I know that you, as a man of your word, will grant."

"And what is that?" asked the President whose mind was starting to sober up and who, realising the rashness of his promise, hoped that the wish would be nothing more than a case of champagne.

"With seventy thousand people as my witnesses I ask you to swap places with me for one day only. Twenty-four hours. You come down to Biarritz for the day and go surfing and I'll be in the Elysée Palace governing France."

"As you wish," said the President.

"Is Thursday suitable?"

"Yes," said the President who thought that one day would be as good (or as bad) as any other.

The new World Champion was not exactly idle over the next few days as he wrote down all the things he wanted to do on the magic day.

Although a constitutionally questionable arrangement, the French were quite relaxed about it since Olivier, like Napoleon after Austerlitz, was the hero of the moment and nobody doubted that the new champion would be an improvement on the wretched incumbent.

Olivier carried out his part of the bargain by leaving his surfboards out for the President in Biarritz. He then flew to Paris on Wednesday night and, in his stylish, new pinstripe suit, made his way to the Elysée, arriving there five minutes before midnight. On the stroke of twelve the President shook hands with his replacement and flew off in the presidential jet for a twenty-four hour rest in Biarritz.

Before entering the Elysée Olivier had taken some speed pills to keep him awake for twenty-four hours as he did not want to waste even a minute of this unique day by sleeping. Five minutes after midnight he was busy with the secretaries issuing his first decrees which, with the help of technology, were able to reach the institutions concerned in time for when they opened in the morning.

His first decree was to release all surfers from prisons except those who were serving sentences for murder and other crimes of violence. However, since the only surfers in prison were there for victimless crimes like drink driving and drugs, the effect of the decree was to release them all.

The second decree removed the TVA tax from surfboards and surf equipment. To make up for any loss of revenue he increased the tax on boogie boards by 300%.

The third decree gave a one day holiday from school for all surfers who wanted to spend the day in the waves.

The fourth decree was to set up a government funded France-U.S.A. sports-friendship scheme of which he and Jared would be the joint presidents. Its purpose was to send sports teams from one country to the other for the purpose of fostering friendship between the French and American people. So happy was he with this that he asked the Principal Private Secretary to put him on the phone to the President at the White House.

The American President was delighted at such a thoughtful gesture and promised an equal amount of funding from the United States. They talked about a lot of things – including state secrets – and at the end of the conversation the man in Washington said how much he looked forward to working in close harmony with the new President.

"But I'm only President for a day," said Olivier.

"Only for a day! Damn. You've talked more sense to me in half an hour than the other President has in seven years."

There were several problems that crossed the presidential desk at the Elysée that morning and one of them was the fate of a group of travelling Western surfers who had been captured by a gang of Moslem terrorists in the southern Philippines the previous week. In the true spirit of the brotherhood of the waves Olivier ordered the Foreign Legion out there to rescue them.

At 11 a.m. he called a meeting of the Cabinet explained to them the hopes and needs of the young people of France and then sacked the four fattest ones on the grounds that they were spending too much of their huge allowances on rich food and wine. "It's for your own good," he explained.

Olivier had always been proud of French achievements – especially the beautiful architecture of Paris – and he had always considered the glass pyramid that President Mitterrand built in the Louvre to be like a carbunkle on the foot. In other words, it should be removed. He ordered in a demolition team and the whole ghastly thing was smashed to pieces by sunset. The Louvre was back to its pristine glory.

Shortly after lunch he was told by his secretary that the President of the European Union was on the phone to talk about farm subsidies, tariff rates and pensions. "Boring! Boring!" he exclaimed and he refused to speak to the insignificant little twit. He was enjoying his day and didn't want to have anything to do with the E.U. which was the all-time downer and, despite the speed, probably would have sent him to sleep. To a wild and radical surfer like Olivier the heavy and oppressive bureaucracy of the E.U. was as alien as the Man in the Moon.

At 2 p.m. he went on national radio and television and told the people of France that, by presidential decree, to-night was National Party Night and that all bars and other places of entertainment could stay open all night. "The French people are full of *joie de vivre* and to-night let us all come together and party on the street, on the beaches, in the parks, in the brothels and in the casinos. We shall never get serious!"

He spent the rest of the day sacking bureaucrats one after the other, thereby slightly lifting the hand of state tyranny that had held the French people in a vice like grip for far too long.

The people loved every minute of it. Here was a man beholden to no special interest group – except surfers whose demands were relatively minor. He could deal with problems effectively and without having to oblige greedy interest groups or pander to particular sections of the voters. For the first time since de Gaulle France had an honest President who was doing the right things. No one spared a thought for the last President spending the day down in Biarritz – not on Olivier's surfboard but in the casino with his mistress. By the end of the day half the population could not even remember his name.

Not surprisingly, there were calls from all over the country for Olivier to remain in the Elysée until the next election; with him at the helm the Fifth Republic didn't look quite so rotten.

Olivier retorted that, sweet as life was at the top, there were no decent waves within three hundred miles of Paris and he had to get back on his board. "I love you France, but see ya."

In fact, he did not even stay in the Elysée until midnight. By ten o'clock he could hear the bands playing in the streets, he could see the fireworks flying through the night and he could smell the sweet scent of partygoers in the air. It was time for him to put aside the affairs of state and to rage. He had turned the whole of France into one big party and he wanted to be part of it.